Religion and *Life Issues*

GCSE Religious Studies for **AQA B**

Lesley Parry, Jan Hayes
and Kim Hands

HODDER
EDUCATION
AN HACHETTE UK COMPANY

Thanks to Hodder for the confidence shown to us in handling the responsibility to write for the new series. Thanks to the teachers who bought the previous books, and made Hodder make that decision – I hope we don't let you down. Thanks to Kate for harassment to write instead of being on the beach! Thanks to the Scrabble-buds for putting up with Kim through this (and the next) book! Seriously, this is a really interesting course (and series), and I hope that students following it will find that too – and be successful in their studies.

Acknowledgements

The Publishers would like to thank the following for permission to reproduce copyright material:

Photo credits

Cover © Don Hammond/Design Pics/Corbis; **p.5** *all* © Lesley Parry; **p.10** *cl* © The Guide Dogs for the Blind Association, *cr* © Lesley Parry; *bl* Kip Rano/Rex Features; *br* © Ann Taylor-Hughes/iStockphoto.com; **p.11** *tr* NBCUPHOTOBANK/ Rex Features, *cl* G.Delpho/WILDLIFE/Still Pictures; **p.12** *t* © Lesley Parry, *c* © Yann Arthus-Bertrand/CORBIS; **p.13** *tl* Julian Makey/Rex Features, *tr* © Lesley Parry, *br* ©David T Gomez/iStockphoto.com; **p.17** *tl* © Stockbyte/Photolibrary Group Ltd, *tc* Pascal Saez/Alamy, *tr* © Photodisc/Getty Images, *bl* © Morley Read/iStockphoto.com, *bc* ©Jim Jurica/ iStockphoto.com, *br* © Lesley Parry; **p.20** *all* © Lesley Parry; **p.22** *tc* ©Photodisc/Getty Images, *tr* © Stockbyte/ Photolibrary Group Ltd; **p.23** © Lesley Parry; **p.24** ©Photodisc/Getty Images; **p.25** © Stockbyte/Photolibrary Group Ltd; **p.27** ©Stockbyte/Photolibrary Group Ltd; **p.33** *t* © Photodisc/Getty Images, *ct* © Lesley Parry, *bl* © Maggie Murray/ Photofusion, *br* © Peter Olive/Photofusion; **p.34** *t* © Con Tanasiuk/Design Pics/Corbis, *c* © Lesley Parry, *b* Andrew Parsons/PA; **p.35** Cate Gillon/Getty Images; **p.36** *t & c* © Lesley Parry, *b* AP Photo/Sergei Grits/PA Photos; **p.37** *tr* Most Wanted/Rex Features, *c* Paul Doyle/Alamy, *rl* Matt Baron/BEI/Rex Features, *bl* Jen Lowery/Rex Features; **p.40** *t* © Flip Schulke/CORBIS, *c* © Bettmann/CORBIS, *b* KPA/Zuma/Rex Features; **p.41** *t* SCANFOTO/PA Photos, *c* © Zen Icknow/ CORBIS, *b* © Jon Hrusa/epa/Corbis; **p.42** *t & c* Dinodia Images/Alamy; **p.45** *tl* CHRISTIAN DARKIN/SCIENCE PHOTO LIBRARY, *tr* DR G. MOSCOSO/SCIENCE PHOTO LIBRARY, *cl* EDELMANN/SCIENCE PHOTO LIBRARY, *cr* Prof Stuart Campbell/Rex Features, *b* © Photodisc/Getty Images; **p.46** *all* © Lesley Parry; **p.58** Peter Macdiarmid/Getty Images; **p.66** Ben Birchall/PA; **p.67** *l* Topical Press Agency/Hulton Archive/Getty Images, *c* © Bettmann/CORBIS, *r* © Bettmann/CORBIS; **p.68** *t* Julian Simmonds/Rex Features, *c* AFP/Getty Images, *b* Richard Wainwright/Corbis; **p.71** *r* DPA/PA Photos, *l* Masatoshi Okauchi/Rex Features; **p.72** © David Pollack/CORBIS; **p.73** © Lesley Parry; **p.75** *t* Jamie Jones/Rex Features, *b* Richard Levine/Alamy; **p.89** © John Walmsley/ www.educationphotos.co.uk; **p.96** © Lesley Parry.

Every effort has been made to trace all copyright holders, but if any have been inadvertently overlooked the Publishers will be pleased to make the necessary arrangements at the first opportunity.

Words highlighted in **bold** are defined in the Glossary on p.102.

Although every effort has been made to ensure that website addresses are correct at time of going to press, Hodder Education cannot be held responsible for the content of any website mentioned in this book. It is sometimes possible to find a relocated web page by typing in the address of the home page for a website in the URL window of your browser.

Hachette UK's policy is to use papers that are natural, renewable and recyclable products and made from wood grown in sustainable forests. The logging and manufacturing processes are expected to conform to the environmental regulations of the country of origin.

Orders: please contact Bookpoint Ltd, 130 Milton Park, Abingdon, Oxon OX14 4SB. Telephone: +44 (0)1235 827720. Fax: +44 (0)1235 400454. Lines are open 9.00–5.00, Monday to Saturday, with a 24-hour message answering service. Visit our website at www.hoddereducation.co.uk.

© Lesley Parry, Jan Hayes and Kim Hands 2009
First published in 2009 by
Hodder Education,
An Hachette UK company
338 Euston Road
London NW1 3BH

Impression number	5 4			
Year	2013	2012	2011	2010

Illustrations by Oxford Illustrators and Richard Duszczak
Typeset in 11 point Minion by DC Graphic Design Limited, Swanley, Kent
Printed in Italy
A catalogue record for this title is available from the British Library

ISBN 978 0 340 98365 2

Contents

Introduction

This book has been written specifically to meet the AQA Specification B Unit 2 course. It follows the Unit outline, moving through the topics in the order of the Unit as set out in the specification. It is informed additionally by the specification from which it grew (also called Specification B).

The Unit is examined through one exam paper of 1 hour and 30 minutes. All six topics within the Unit will be represented on that paper, though candidates will be required to answer questions on only four topics. Each question being worth 18 marks, and with quality of written response now within the mark scheme itself (rather than an additional sum), the total for the paper will be 72 marks. An example of the paper and what it should look like is found in Appendix II at the back of this book. This is annotated to help demystify the exam language and paper style.

Unit 2, when studied in conjunction with a second Unit, leads to a full GCSE qualification.

The topics within the book cover the Unit content from a variety of angles, as well as providing the necessary information required by those studying for the exam. Each topic asks students to think about what they are being told, and about the implications of the issues. There are many opportunities for evaluation work, which now forms 50 per cent of the total mark for the exam. Knowledge and understanding of the topics are important, but ability to apply that knowledge is vital to achieve the highest grades. The style of text is designed to encourage and develop exactly that.

Exam technique is a constant theme, as it can cost candidates many marks if poor. It is worth using class time to teach/learn good techniques via the mechanics of good answers. The authors of this book are all Senior Examiners with AQA, and have lengthy experience in their roles. They give good advice, so make good use of it!

The specification allows centres to prepare candidates to answer from one or more religious traditions on any question. This book allows study of a single religious tradition, or of several – all religious traditions are commented on for each element within each topic.

Given this is an issues course, students should be encouraged to collect their own examples of the issues as met in the news. They can collect, add comments, give their own opinion, and even try to say what they think religion(s) would say. This will help with their recall and provide real examples to call on in the exam.

A revision outline in Appendix I is designed to support revision, but can act as a checklist for students as they move through the course.

About this course

This course gets you to think about six key modern-day issues. Some of them will have directly affected you, or you will have direct experience of them. Some you will know of through other people's experience. Some you may only know of through the media. Keep in mind that you already have a whole load of knowledge about these issues, and you can use that in your exam.

For the exam, you have to answer questions on four of the topics. All six topics will always be on the exam paper – you just answer four. Actually, you could answer more, because they'll still get marked, and the four best answered questions get taken forward as your marks. BUT – people who do this, often don't get great marks. It is only ever a good idea if you have finished answering – at *your* right speed (not having rushed) – and still have loads of time left.

As you go through the issues, you will have opinions and attitudes to them. That is good! You will be asked about your own opinion on many of the issues as part of the exam. So do take the chances to discuss and explain your own opinions – it helps you present them better in the exam when you have to.

Keep your eye on the news – there will be lots of stories that link to these issues in the time it takes to do this course. Those stories could figure in exam papers, which are written about fifteen months before you get to sit the exam, often using topical stories. They certainly give you a wider range of examples to use in your answers when you are trying to explain or back up a point you make. Could it be the time to start a scrapbook?!

The religious bit

Religion also has opinions on all these issues. This is an RE course after all, so you are going to see the attitudes of some religions. You will have to write about them in the exam if you want to get good grades. This means trying to understand what those attitudes are and where they come from – in other words, the beliefs and teachings of the religions. In this book, you'll be given a small number of beliefs and teachings for each religion on each topic. Quite often you can use these teachings in a few different topics (which always helps!). If a teaching will apply to more than one topic – use it.

This double page gives you some general teachings, which you can apply to all the different topics. It cuts down the number of teachings you have to learn, and means you can understand these thoroughly. However, the best answers in exams always use beliefs and teachings that are specific to the topics, as well as the general ones. Don't forget to learn some of these when you meet them later, as well. Mark this page, or copy these teachings into the front of your book or file. Then use them as the basis for your work. When you study a topic, refer back to these to help you work out what the attitude will be to that topic.

Buddhism

1   Reincarnation and **karma** – our words, thoughts and deeds create energies that shape our future rebirths. We need to make sure these are positive.
2   The Five Precepts (guidelines for living). These are – not harming others (**ahimsa**); using language kindly; not taking what is not freely given; not clouding our minds; no sexual misconduct.
3   Compassion (loving kindness).

Christianity

1   **Jesus'** two key teachings – Love God; Love your neighbour.
2   Equality of all, because in Genesis we are told that God made each of us.
3   Justice (fairness) – since everyone is equal, everyone deserves fairness.
4   Forgiveness and love are ideas taught by Jesus, and shown in his actions.

Hinduism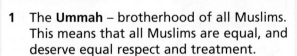

Hindu holy books list many virtues. These include –

1   ahimsa (non-violence)
2   self-discipline
3   tolerance
4   service to others
5   compassion
6   providing shelter/support to others
7   respect for all life
8   wisdom
9   honesty with others and oneself
10 cleanliness.

Islam

1   The **Ummah** – brotherhood of all Muslims. This means that all Muslims are equal, and deserve equal respect and treatment.
2   That everyone has to follow duties set by **Allah** (God), for example, the Five Pillars.
3   **Shari'ah Law**, which is Muslim law stemming from the **Qur'an** and Hadith, and applied to modern life by Islamic scholars.

Judaism ♉

The Ten Commandments are found in the Book of Genesis in the Torah.

1 Love only G-d.
2 Make no idols of G-d.
3 Do not take G-d's name in vain.
4 Keep the Sabbath holy.
5 Respect your parents.
6 Do not kill.
7 Do not steal.
8 Do not commit adultery.
9 Do not tell lies.
10 Do not be jealous of what others have.

Sikhism ☬

The **Khalsa** vows.

1 Meditation and service to the One God, including worship, following the teachings, and wearing the 5Ks as a mark of the faith and devotion to it.
2 Do not use intoxicants.
3 Do not eat meat that has been ritually slaughtered (most Sikhs are **vegetarians**).
4 Equality of all people, leading to respect for all and a desire to fight injustice, and including not hurting others by theft or deed.

Sikh ethical virtues – sharing with others, including tithing (sewa); dutifulness; prudence; justice; tolerance; temperance; chastity; patience; contentment; detachment and humility.

Task

Choose a religion (or two) and, using the teachings from the religion(s) on these pages, try to work out what a believer's attitude might be to the following:

a   abortion (the deliberate termination of a pregnancy)
b   dog fighting
c   declaring war on a neighbouring country because your country wants their goldmines/reserves
d   how you should treat people who are different from you.

Topic One Religion and animal rights

This topic starts the course, and will start the exam paper. It has always been a popular exam choice on other courses, so let's enjoy it. We need to check out – the different ways humans use animals; the rights and wrongs of that usage; the status and rights animals (should) have; and what the religions think about the use of animals.

How do we make use of animals?

On this page, there are lots of ideas of how humans use and interact with animals. You could be asked about specific uses of animals as well as attitudes generally.

Let's take some time to think of the ways humans use animals – with a partner, come up with a list. Now decide which ones are good for us, and which are good for the animals. Are any of them exploitation? In other words, do humans take advantage of animals? Why do you think this happens?

What rights do animals have?

Have a look at this attitude-line, which gives answers to this question from one extreme to the other – where are you, and why?

Revision Tips

As you go through this course, collect stories and images from newspapers and the internet. These give you real examples to use in your answers. They give you images to help remember. They also give you a chance to ask yourself what the religion(s) you are studying would say about the situations. This reinforces what you have learned, especially if you make notes with the clippings you take.

Any of the attitudes on the line could be the statement you have to argue about in evaluative questions on the exam. Let's think them through – for each attitude, try to give some reasons and examples why a person might say them.

> None at all – humans are superior to all other species, so we can do what we want.

> We should treat the animals we need with respect, but can do what we want with the others.

> Some animals deserve more respect than humans do.

> Some animals should have more rights than others.

> All species are equal – human, animal, insect, bird, the lot.

> All animals should be given more rights than humans – they were here first.

Research Task

There are lots of **animal rights** organisations, many of which have websites. The following give religious attitudes to the status of animals, and lots of information about the issues to do with animal rights and our use of animals. Write a report on one of the websites – its accessibility, presentation, and how clear the info is. Then check out the religions you are studying from the notes it has.

www.animalaid.org.uk

www.animalethics.org

www.animalsuffering.com/religion.html

Now you know what we are trying to do in this topic.

Humans and animals

Can you imagine a world without animals? Even those we ignore can do vital jobs – wild bees pollinate plants and trees making sure that they continue to produce foods for us to eat.

Animals help us – pulling carts, for example. They give us companionship – have you got pets? They are part of our diet – we eat them. Parts of animals are used in clothing, and other types of manufacturing. They entertain us in **zoos** and circuses. We learn from them – in how they live and behave, as well as by experimenting on them. Birdsong and whale song can both soothe us when we feel tense. Many films and cartoons have animals as their focus and we take pleasure in that.

We also overwork animals – causing their death. We experiment on them, taking them away from their natural environments and killing them during or after those experiments. We buy them as pets, then mistreat them. We hunt them in cruel ways, sometimes just for our own enjoyment, not because we need anything. If an animal is in the way of a human project, it has to move, or die. We eat animals, usually produced on farms that are more like factories and which treat the animals like products not as living beings.

Every so often, we hear of animals that have killed humans or hurt them – like a shark attack, or a dog biting someone. Some species are dying out, so plans to build are sometimes affected by where those species live. If you have ever had a kitten, it's not so easy to litter-train at first! Not all of them like us – they bite and sting. And why on earth are there wasps?!

> What is the relationship between humans and animals – which side gets the best deal?

Are we different?

> So what does make us different?

Well, most humans think they are superior to animals. The fact that we eat animals, but kill an animal that eats a person, suggests that we think we are superior. We also make animals do things we'd never ask of a human – for example, the US marines now have dolphins that have been trained to seek and lay underwater mines. This suggests that we think they are less valuable than us.

Humans use reason and logic to work things out; animals seem to behave more out of instinct. Our technology is more advanced than any used by animals. Our ways of communicating are more complicated. Some religions also believe that God gave humans dominion (power) over animals, which has been interpreted to mean 'do as you like', at times.

Religions call animals '**sentient beings**' – creatures that have senses and can feel pain. They are either created by God deliberately (Christianity, Islam, Judaism and Sikhism), or are beings in the cycle of rebirth (Buddhism and Hinduism). In all cases, they have value. No religion says we can't use animals, but they all say we should treat them with respect.

The Basics

1 List some ways we use animals.
2 How are animals and humans different?
3 Why should religious people 'care for' animals?
4 **People should show animals more respect**. What do you think? Explain your reasons.

 Now you have thought about differences

Introducing the elements of this topic

This topic isn't just about how we use and treat animals. The examiner is going to ask you about specific ways we use and treat animals. He or she might ask you to describe or compare those ways, and to explain the issues caused by each. They will certainly want you to be able to write about a range of ways, and bring ideas from all of those into your exam answers – especially for the evaluative answers. So the next few pages are going to take each way that is listed in the course information, and make you think about it.

The bits to learn

- A definition/description of each, including an example.
- Why some people might see them as good.
- Why some people might see them as bad.
- What the religions might say.

Have a look at the uses of animals that the course mentions. Do you understand what each is about? Go through them, and write down, or discuss with your partner/group what you know. See if you can already say something for each of those **bits to learn** about each of the elements listed below.

- Saving animals from extinction.
- Animals as companions.
- Animals in sport.
- Transport and work animals.
- Farming of animals.
- Zoos.

- **Hunting**.
- Bull fighting.
- The fur and ivory trades.
- **Genetic modification** of animals.
- Cloning animals.
- Treatment of wildlife.

What the religions say

You already know that they think animals were either specially made, or are part of the same cycle of rebirth that humans are in. This gives them a special status. Even if we believe humans are better or superior, animals still have value. From that we can guess that if we abuse animals in how we use them or treat them, there might be a consequence.

Well, let's look more closely at what the religions say. You can then apply their attitudes each time you meet an element. This is a really good way to reinforce the knowledge in your head, and so have a clear idea about their attitudes to animals overall.

From the next few pages, choose the religion(s) you have studied, and make notes on their religious attitudes to animals. You need to note:

- an overview of each religion's attitude to animals. (Christians think animals were…)
- three to five teachings to use in exams. (The **Bible** says 'God created everything'.)
- an explanation of how each teaching applies to the issue of animals. (When the Bible says 'God created everything', that includes animals, so they must be special.)

 Now you know what this topic is about

Religious attitudes to animal use

Buddhism

Buddhism teaches compassion and non-violence. Intention behind any act is very important; if it is not compassionate, bad karma will result. Animals are part of the whole cycle of rebirth, and have a future as a human. It is important to show respect to all life.

Buddhism teaches:

- So long as sentient beings suffer, I will be there to help as much as I can (Bodhisattva's Vow).
- To not hurt other sentient beings (First Precept).
- Right Livelihood includes not having a job that exploits animals.
- All living things fear being put to death. Putting oneself in the place of another, let no one kill nor cause another to kill (Dhammapada).
- In some of his many lifetimes, the **Buddha** gave up his life to help animals.

Buddhist attitudes often come down to intention – why you do something. Do it for a positive reason, compassion, for example, and it is good, so long as the good outweighs any **suffering**. Do it for a negative reason, greed, for example, and it is bad. All this generates good or bad karma and that is what shapes our future lifetime(s).

Buddhists should try not to harm other beings. They should not have jobs or roles that causes suffering. They should also show respect to animals (as sentient beings) in any situation.

This doesn't mean they can't kill or eat animals; many Buddhists around the world do. Some monks will only eat meat if it is offered to them as alms. A Buddhist would accept the killing of an animal in pain or suffering where there was no other option. For sport, it is always wrong.

Christianity ✝

Christians believe that God gave humans dominion over the world and all in it. This gives them license to use it as they wish, bearing in mind that God wants them to look after the world (**stewardship**), and will expect it back in good condition on **Judgement Day**.

Christianity teaches:

- God made the world and gave humans dominion over it (Genesis).
- 'Scientists must abandon laboratories and factories of death' (Pope John Paul II).
- Animals are a part of God's **creation** and as such deserve respect and protection (St Francis of Assisi).
- Jesus said that God cares about even the sparrows.
- The earth and everything in it is the Lord's (Bible).

Christians believe that because all life was created by God, it should be protected and looked after. The developed world, which is mainly Christian, is the biggest consumer of meat, has many battery farms, sees hunting as a sport, and leads the world in using animals in medical research. At the same time, its zoos commonly protect endangered species, most families have pets, and animals are used as support for humans – police horses, guide dogs for the blind, and so on. Many Christians today choose to eat organic and free range meat, if they are not vegetarian. Many actively campaign against hunting as sport. Many agree only with the use of animals in medical experiments, and encourage research in methods that do not use animals. There is a dilemma. For many Christians, use of animals is acceptable if they have been looked after well – humane treatment is the key.

On the Day of Judgement, they believe they will be called to account for their actions including how they treated animals, and if they fought or supported the systems that cause animals to suffer.

Let's debate! There are statements at the bottom of the next few pages for you to discuss in groups. Write each statement on a big sheet of paper, each group adds the points they think of. Swap the sheets until everyone has seen each point. If you agree with a point, tick it. If you disagree, put a cross and a reason why.

Hinduism ॐ

Respect for all life is central to Hinduism. All forms of life have the spark of the divine within them – the Ultimate Reality, **Brahman**. Most Hindus are vegetarians, and certain animals are considered very sacred in India, for example, cows and monkeys. The law of karma guides people's behaviour, so hurting animals would go against that.

Hinduism teaches:

- Avoid harming other sentient beings or forms of life (ahimsa).
- Hindu worship includes respect for all of nature, and many deities are linked to specific animals, for example, Shiva and the cobra.
- By avoiding any harm to animals or to nature, humans will come to be ready for eternal life (Laws of Manu).
- 'On a Brahmin…cow…elephant…dog… person of low caste, wise men look with equal eye' (Bhagavad Gita).
- It is a duty of the grihasta (householder) stage of life to feed animals.

Respect for animals is key to Hindu life. At times animals are almost worshipped, for example, cows, the temple elephants, and monkeys. Animals are part of the cycle of reincarnation.

Factory farming is seen as cruel and disrespectful. In the West, we send animals no longer good for farming to slaughterhouses. In contrast, there are retirement homes for cows in India.

Causing suffering to other beings can never be justified, even for medicine, so any kind of animal experimentation is wrong. This also means that any sport, like bull fighting, which causes suffering, is wrong.

In the Ramayana, Rama goes hunting. This may be taken to say that hunting for food is acceptable. Since every action gains us good or bad karma, Hindus have to weigh up what they do as to whether it helps or hinders them in future. The way they treat animals is part of this.

> People who mistreat pets should be jailed.

> Zoos should all be closed down, and the animals released.

Islam ☪

Allah created the world and all in it. Each human is a **khalifah** (steward) – and has a duty to look after Allah's creation. People's success in carrying out that duty will be assessed on Judgement Day, when everyone has to account for all their life's deeds before Allah. Using animals is fine, but you have to be able to show you treated them fairly.

Islam teaches:

- Humans are khalifah – trustees of the world, and its guardians (Qur'an).
- Nature has been made inferior to humans, and can be used to improve the well-being of people and society.
- **Muhammad** (pbuh) insisted animals be well-treated, given adequate food and rest, and if any are to be slaughtered, it is to be done in the most humane way possible (**Sunnah**).
- Showing kindness to an animal is an act that is rewarded by Allah (Sunnah).
- If a man unjustly kills any animal, he will be accused by the animal in front of Allah on Judgement Day (Sunnah).

For Muslims humans are superior to animals. However, they must be looked after properly, not exploited or abused. Prophet Muhammad (pbuh) was very clear about this, and there are many stories where he criticises people for their treatment of animals, or praises others. One story tells how he cut a piece out of his cloak, which was being used by a cat and her kittens, rather than disturb them.

Farming is important as it helps to feed people. However, in battery farms, animals do not get proper care or rest, which makes them haram. These farms usually send their animals to slaughterhouses, making the meat haram, because the killing isn't done following Shari'ah Law.

Experimentation has been very important in medical advances, but duplicate trials, and non-medical testing are an abuse of our power as khalifah. It is better to experiment without animals.

Hunting is a sport in many Muslim countries, though the meat caught is usually eaten. Many sports involving animals are frowned upon, because of cruelty – like bull fighting.

Judaism

G-d created the world and all in it, giving dominion over everything to man. Stewardship (the duty to look after G-d's creation in its entirety) is important in Judaism. Animals are inferior to humans, and can be used by them, but must always be treated well.

Judaism teaches:

- G-d made the world and all in it. He gave humans dominion over all (Genesis).
- A righteous man looks after his animals (Proverbs – Ketuvim).
- On the Sabbath Day, do no work, nor your animals (Torah).
- Animals must be treated with respect because they are G-d's creation, but human life will always have more value than animal life.
- Do not be cruel to animals (**Noachide Laws**).

Judaism has a duty to help and improve the well-being of others. This will involve the use and death of animals. However, any form of cruelty is wrong, and there are many laws within the 613 Mitzvot about looking after animals. These include giving them time to rest, adequate food and shelter, not causing them unnecessary suffering, and not making them work too hard.

As part of G-d's creation, and for our use, we can use them as we wish – to help us, for example guide dogs, police dogs, animals of burden – all are acceptable, as long as they are treated well.

Farming is about providing food for people, and we need food to live.

Hunting is forbidden by Jewish law. It is seen as unnecessary to people's needs, and a cause of cruelty. Any meat from an animal that has been hunted is treyfah (unfit).

Animal experiments are only acceptable as long as they are for the advancement of medical science, because they help to improve the well-being of humans. However, replica trials, and those tests that involve cruelty are forbidden.

Sikhism

All is the creation of God, and all life has within it the light of God. Sikhs should respect God's creation as a way of worshipping God. There are no clear teachings on certain things, and Sikhs are expected to act according to their own conscience, so for example whilst many Sikhs are vegetarian, some choose not to be.

Sikhism teaches:

- If you say that there is God in every being, then why kill a chicken? (Guru Granth Sahib.)
- God's light pervades every creature, and every creature is contained within his light (Guru Granth Sahib).
- In the **langar**, only vegetarian food is served. Many Sikhs are vegetarian out of respect for God's creation.
- All food is pure, for God has given it for our sustenance (Adi Granth).
- I enjoyed myself on the banks of the River Jumna…I hunted many tigers, deer and bears (Guru Gobind Singh).

For Sikhs, the facts that God created everything, and that they have a duty to worship God through sewa, should mean they treat everything in the world around them with respect. So, any exploitation of, or cruelty to, animals would be wrong. Indeed, they are forbidden to eat halal meat because the slaughter method is considered cruel.

Farms are important to produce the quantities of food people need to eat. Those farms where treatment of animals is poor are unacceptable.

The Gurus enjoyed hunting, so it is not forbidden. However, a distinction is made between the hunting the Gurus did, and hunting like bear-baiting, which is just cruel. The use of traps would also be wrong, as it is undoubtedly cruel.

Experiments for medical purposes help to improve the life of others, and so can be justified. Replica experiments, and those for testing products such as make-up are seen as wrong. Many Sikhs work in the medical system as a form of sewa.

We've learnt most of our medicine from animal research, so it must continue.

Animal sports are fine because they entertain people.

This topic, your notes

Companions and helpers

Surveys tell us that 43 per cent of households in the UK have at least one pet. As societies get richer, more people keep animals as pets rather than working animals. Our pets seem to get a different status to other animals – we think of them differently. I bet you'd never have a pig sleep on the end of your bed, but you let your cat or dog! These animals are our 'friends' and companions – many people regard their pet with love.

There are many animals that help us, as well as being companions – guide dogs for the blind and hearing dogs for the deaf, for example. These specially trained animals help blind or deaf people be independent. Without them, life would be difficult.

Task

For each topic on pages 10–11, design a slide show. It must include:

• an explanation of what the topic is, including images
• information about a linked organisation (check the internet)
• a list of the benefits/pros
• a list of the problems/cons
• what you think the religion(s) you have studied would say about it, using teachings to back up your ideas.

Have you got a pet? How do you look after it? Does it help you? Is it your friend? Would you eat it, or experiment on it, or lock it up all its life with no exercise?

Transport and work

Humans have always used animals to help them work. We also use them to find drugs and explosives, to catch fish (cormorant fishing in Japan) and as vehicles. These animals are well looked after, even after they have been 'retired'. Many families own animals that provide them with food, and help them work their land. However, many animals are 'beasts of burden', spending their lives carrying huge loads, and eventually being left to die because they can no longer work.

Some of the issues:

- This is not their natural life – necessary training is often harsh.
- Many beasts of burden are not fed or rested properly, and suffer all their lives.

Farming

Farming is the business of agriculture. Nearly all the food we eat has come from farms.

Most people in developing countries have very small farms with few animals. They are farming for their own family, selling any extra at a market. In the UK, we see battery, organic, and free-range farms. Supermarkets sell meat from all these types of farms.

Some of the issues:

- Animals are not cared for properly because they are just products.
- Animals are forced to breed at unnatural rates.
- Nature versus profit – farming is a business.

In sport

horse racing…greyhound racing… dog fighting…badger baiting

In many sports, animals are highly trained and well looked after. Mistreatment leads to punishments. However, many sports involve animals fighting against each other – like dog fighting and cricket fighting. These are considered cruel in many societies and can be illegal (such as dog fighting in the UK). None of these sports are how the animal would naturally live.

Some of the issues:

◆ It is cruel to make two animals fight.
◆ Even well-kept animals can just be slaughtered when they are no longer 'good enough'.
◆ The animals get injured.

Hunting

Hunting is when we chase and kill an animal. It could be for food, for fur, or for sport. In the UK, many enjoy it as a blood sport.

Some of the issues:

> *Hunting for meat for your family is okay, I think. I don't agree with shooting a load of birds or animals when you don't need the food.*
> — **Jade**

> *I have seen some of the traps they use for hunting – horrible. The animals die slowly in agony. Some even try to bite their own limbs off to escape. My dog died in one of those traps – they don't just catch wild animals, see.*
> — **Jen**

Bullfighting

Bullfighting is the national sport of Spain. It is also found in Portugal, parts of France and in some South American countries. The matador uses set moves during the different parts of a fight with the bull(s) to distract, annoy and hurt it. Finally, it should be killed by one well-aimed sword stab through the heart.

Some of the issues:

◆ It is obviously cruel.
◆ The bull dies in great pain over a long time.
◆ Even when a bull is spared, few survive their journey back to their ranch because of poor treatment of fight injuries.

> *What other sports use animals? Do the animals have training? Are there any sports which you think are worse than others for the animals? Can you name any 'blood sports'?*

> *In hunting we chase an animal just for the thrill of the chase, and then, when it is too tired to escape, we let hunting animals tear it apart. That is wrong.*
> — **Jim**

> *Tigers are nearly extinct, but are still hunted for medicine. They'll have to find other medicines when they've killed them all, so why not find them now?*
> — **Brad**

Now you know about some sports uses of animals   11

Task

For each topic on pages 12–13, design a poster. It must include:

- an explanation of what the topic is, including images
- information about a linked organisation (check the internet)
- a list of the benefits/pros
- a list of the problems/cons
- what you think the religion(s) you have studied would say about it, using teachings to back up your ideas.

Experimentation

Animal experiments further our medical knowledge, test new drugs, or test new products for harmfulness (toxicity). Medical science has always used animals. For example, many surgical procedures were perfected on animals. Some experiments just mean a change in diet, others do cause injury and even death. At the end of the experimentation any live animals are humanely destroyed. Since 1986, there have been specific laws to control experimentation.

The animals – mainly guinea pigs, mice, rats, rabbits, dogs and monkeys – are specially bred in farms.

Some of the issues:

- It is cruel. Even scientists accept the animals suffer – though for greater good.
- There are other alternatives, such as using tissue cultures.
- Animal genetics and human genetics are different, and often reactions are not the same.

Zoos

Zoos are places where animals are kept for people to look at. Most animals are from other countries and climates, not the country the zoo is in. Zoos in rich countries do try to recreate conditions for the animals – they have specially shaped and built compounds, and their food is particular to their natural diet. Zoos in developing countries are not usually like this.

Many zoos are involved in programmes such as helping to re-establish endangered species.

Some of the issues:

- The animals are not in their natural environment.
- Animals in all zoos are caged over night every night (often their most active time in the wild).
- Breeding programmes are very expensive.

Genetic modification and cloning

This is about taking the DNA of an animal, changing it and creating new forms of the species. Scientists have been able to change the DNA of one species of pig, for example, so that its kidneys can be used in human transplants.

Cloning is when scientists make an exact replica of something by inserting its DNA into an embryo. This is then replanted into an animal's womb to develop. Most famous is Dolly the Sheep (scientists needed 277 attempts; she lived for six years). This could be a way to save some endangered species.

Some of the issues:

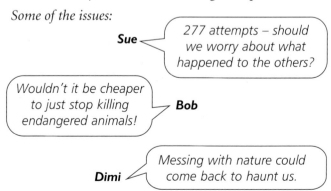

Sue: *277 attempts – should we worry about what happened to the others?*

Bob: *Wouldn't it be cheaper to just stop killing endangered animals!*

Dimi: *Messing with nature could come back to haunt us.*

The fur and ivory trades

Fur usually comes from farms that use battery methods to breed thousands of animals, and then electrocute them so as to not damage the pelt/fur. Many of the farms are in countries like Korea, which is hot, whilst the animal is originally from a very cold country.

Ivory comes from elephants, which are killed for their tusks. It is an illegal trade across the world, though many people own ivory objects. It was very fashionable in the nineteenth and twentieth centuries.

Some of the issues:

◆ We don't *need* fur or ivory.
◆ Fur farms are very cruel.
◆ Ivory poaching has endangered whole species of elephant.

Treatment of animals in the wild

> *Do you get birds in your garden?
> Do you feed them? What other wild animals
> do you see? How do you react when you see
> wild animals – fear, curiosity, awe?*

We see wild animals every day, and mainly ignore them. Where they come near we often chase them away or kill them, think of foxes and rats.

Many of these species are endangered. They all have an important role in the ecosystem, and many provide obvious beauty to our environment.

Some of the issues:

◆ Whose space is the world – ours or theirs or both?
◆ Are we endangering too many species?
◆ Should we support wildlife more through feeding etc?

Preventing extinction of animals

Extinction of a species is when surveys and investigations and other counts all fail to find any example of a species over a period of time. Humans have already made many species extinct. Scientists reckon over 15,000 species are currently known to be endangered (we don't know every species that exists). Once a species is extinct it is gone forever.

Some of the issues:

◆ All species have a key role in the ecosystem.
◆ The species we lose could be helpful to medicine or research.
◆ Do we have a right to do this, for example hunting tigers to extinction for fun?
◆ Our children won't see these creatures – they will inherit a depleted world.

Research Task

Find out more about animal rights. Check out the work of these groups – RSPCA, IFAW, PETA, National Anti-Vivisection Society. You can learn more about the issues as these groups see them, and the ways in which these groups campaign for change.
Check out **www.beep.ac.uk** – the Bio-Ethics Education Project. It has lots of good information about how we treat animals and the environment.

Vegetarianism

There are many reasons why people are vegetarian. These are usually to do with health, upbringing, religion and concerns about farming methods. Some people eat no meat or dairy products at all (vegans); some choose to eat no meat or meat products (vegetarian).

The Christian, Muslim and Jewish faiths all allow meat in their diets. Some Christians fast at certain times of year. Muslims and Jews may not eat certain meats, and must only eat ritually slaughtered meat (called halal for Muslims, kosher for Jews). This reflects the idea that God/Allah/G-d gave humans dominion over animals, and so they could be used by humans, including as food. Hindus and Buddhists, on the whole, are vegetarian, reflecting two important beliefs – ahimsa (non-violence) and respect for all life. Many Sikhs are vegetarian to show respect for God's creation, and the Sikh langar always serves a vegetarian meal.

The Basics

1. Check back to pages 7–9 to find the one or two religions you have studied. For each, write the important teachings to do with animals. Add any other ideas you have come across in your studies (for example, that God created all life).
2. Use what you have written to write a paragraph on the attitude of each of your one or two religions to animals.
3. Re-use those teachings to explain the attitude of each to eating meat.
4. Why do people choose to be vegetarian?
5. **Eating meat is disrespectful to God's creation**. Do you agree? Give reasons and explain your answer, showing you have thought about more than one point of view.

Research Task

Find out about the dietary requirements of followers of the religion(s) you have studied.

Now you have thought about eating meat, and attitudes to it

Exam practice

Introducing half the exam – AO1 questions

Half of the exam marks are for a certain type of question. This tests what you can remember from what you have learnt. It is the kind of question that asks you what something means, or why some people do something, or what the religions think about something.

Questions use these command words:

Give...	Write the name of something, or one reason why something happens. The mark tells you how many different things the examiner wants to know – if the question doesn't tell you that. So, *Give ways in which people use animals. (2 marks)*, wants two ways.
Name...	Write the name of something. This could be its proper name, like Bible, or could be what it is, like *holy book*.
Explain briefly...	For this, you have to write something, and then say a bit more about what you have just written. *Give* and *Name* only want one detail – the most basic information. *Explain* wants more. When it uses the word *briefly*, it is to try to stop you from writing everything you know. So it is an answer, with a bit extra. This is usually used on two and three mark questions.
Explain...	So, if *Explain briefly* wants an answer with a bit extra, *Explain* wants two or three different answers, and a couple of those with a bit extra. There is a bit more depth to your answer – you'll do better if you develop an idea by giving two extra bits of information. These questions are usually worth 4 or 5 marks.

In the exam, there are six questions – one for each topic in this book. Each one is worth 18 marks – split equally between this kind of question and evaluative questions (ones where you have to argue about a statement being true or not). So it is important to be able to do well on these questions.

Try one of each of those *commands* in these questions:

1 **Give** two ways in which humans use animals. (2 marks)

2 **Name** two kinds of sport involving animals. (2 marks)

3 **Explain briefly** why some religious believers choose not to eat meat. (3 marks)

4 **Explain** the attitudes of the religion(s) you have studied to experiments on live animals. (6 marks)

Now go back through the work you have done in this topic. Write a set of questions using these command words for a partner – see if they can answer them. They can do the same for you – it is a way of revising and organising the ideas in your head.

Questions about attitudes to animals

How confident are you about explaining the religious attitude to animals, or to how we treat them? Do you think you can say enough to get 4 or 5 marks for each religion? It isn't so tough an ask – three teachings in your answer, each with a bit of explanation, should do it.

What about the specific bits that made up this topic? How confident are you on bull fighting, genetic modification and so on? Could you say what the religions think? Not so easy, perhaps.

Actually, it is straightforward because you know their attitude to animals. You can use your intelligence to apply that to the specific topics and the problems they cause. Follow this formula, and then practise some:

First, know a definition for each issue. *What do we mean each time?*

Second, know some of the main problems each issue causes. *What is the big deal?*

Third, know the attitude of the religion to animals generally. *What is the general attitude to animals?*

Fourth, apply that attitude to each issue by way of the main problems. *What does the attitude make them say?*

There are some generalisations in answering this. Religions usually talk about:

* life being sacred (**sanctity of life**)
* the world being God's creation
* us having a role in looking after the world and its animals.

So, ask yourself – does the issue conflict or agree with any of these general ideas? Use them as your starter in explaining the attitude. Make sure you state the topic in your answer, so that your answer can't be read as a broad answer.

Let's see an example…

Explain religious attitudes to making animals extinct. Use beliefs and teachings in your answer. (6 marks)

The FORMULA	The ANSWER
First, explain what it means.	Making animals extinct is when there are no more of a species left alive in the world.
Second, what are the main problems?	This means that the food chain is affected. It also means that no one can see that animal ever again.
Third, what is the religion's attitude to animals?	Christianity (or Islam or Judaism or Sikhism or Hinduism) believes God created animals, so they are special. God gave humans the responsibility to look after them and the world (stewardship), and doing so is an act of worship of God, as well as appreciation.
Fourth, what does the attitude make them say about the issue?	So, by making animals extinct, we destroy God's creation. This is not what stewardship means, and is disrespectful to God.

Actually in exams students struggle most with questions they have never had a chance to practise, so they aren't used to the way it is worded, or the actual topic asked. Any work you do – even with a book full of notes in front of you – helps. It lets your brain see the question, and think about exactly that kind of a question. When you see that type again in the exam, your brain doesn't panic as much, so you can get on with it.

Okay, you need to practise. Try using the formula with these, then try any other from this topic:

a Using animals in work.

b Hunting animals.

Topic Two Religion and planet earth

World Summit agrees targets for reduction of emissions

More medicine finds in rainforest

Big increase in environmentally friendly holidays

'Green' schemes appearing all over globe

ENVIRONMENTAL FILM WATCHED BY MILLIONS

SCHOOLS TEACH ENVIRONMENTAL VALUES

This topic is about the environment and, from the religions' point of view, humanity's duty to look after the environment. It considers the situation the modern world is in, and how governments are trying to tackle issues.

How do we treat our world?
Well, or badly? Can you give some examples?
Should we treat it better? Why?

Some key ideas include:

- Life is special or sacred. This means all life, not just human life. Humans have a duty or responsibility to look after it.
- Humans have a responsibility to look after the world – for God, for themselves, for other people now and in the future.
- Everybody has a role to play in looking after the natural world – not just some people.

The Basics

1. List some of the ways we damage our world.
2. Split your list into the ways individuals damage the world, and how companies might damage the world.
3. What responsibility do individuals have for looking after the environment? What about governments?
4. What makes it difficult to look after the environment? Give examples to show what you mean more clearly (think on different scales – at school, in your home street, in the country, across the world).

The origins of life

This course is interested in how life began. We can take the scientific route, which is a theory based on bits of evidence. Or we can take the religious route, which is stories based on what people say God told them – whichever you choose to accept as your *truth* is fine, but you still need to know both for the exam.

How the world began

The Big Bang Theory says:

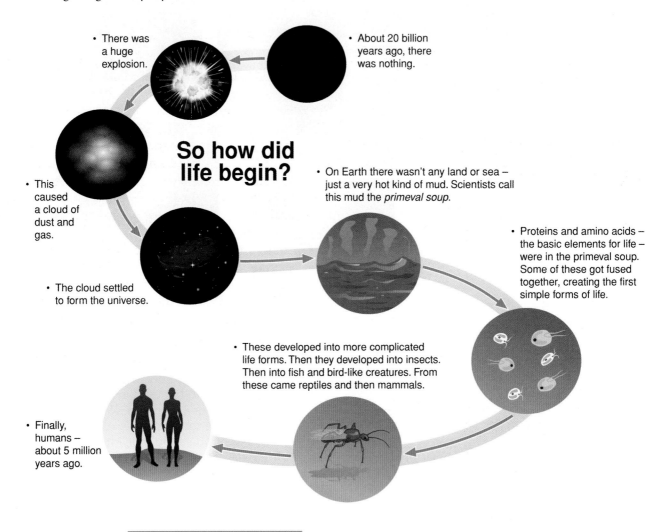

- There was a huge explosion.

- About 20 billion years ago, there was nothing.

- This caused a cloud of dust and gas.

- The cloud settled to form the universe.

So how did life begin?

- On Earth there wasn't any land or sea – just a very hot kind of mud. Scientists call this mud the *primeval soup*.

- Proteins and amino acids – the basic elements for life – were in the primeval soup. Some of these got fused together, creating the first simple forms of life.

- These developed into more complicated life forms. Then they developed into insects. Then into fish and bird-like creatures. From these came reptiles and then mammals.

- Finally, humans – about 5 million years ago.

The Basics

1 Explain in your own words how science says the universe began.
2 Explain in your own words how science says life began.
3 Think about these ideas – why do some people disagree with them?
4 **Science explains everything we need to know.** Do you agree? Give reasons and explain your answer.

Now you know the scientific beliefs about how life began

What the religions say

Religions each have their own ideas about how the world and life began. They are almost always linked to a God, and this gives religions a special attitude to the world around them. They feel responsible for the world because of their beliefs.

Creation

Christianity, ✝ Islam ☪ and Judaism ✡ share the same story of how the world began. At the beginning of time, God created the world from nothing. It took six 'days', and after its completion God was pleased with it. The creation included the world (land, sea, vegetation, sun, moon, stars) and all life on it (fish, birds and animals). Humans were the final creation.

Hindus ॐ believe that Brahman is responsible for the universe. There are many creation stories in Hinduism. In one, Vishnu is said to sleep on a cobra in the middle of a vast ocean of nothingness. Vishnu wakes, and from his navel grows a lotus flower. Inside the lotus is Brahma, who creates the world. Shiva is also there, and he is responsible for the cycle of life and death in all of the creation.

Sikhism ☬ also believes that God created the world – everything comes from God, and without God nothing exists. God is the one who maintains life, so that it continues to exist.

Stewardship

This means 'looking after'. All religions believe we have to look after the world. It belongs to God, not us. By looking after the world, we show respect to God. In fact, in Islam ☪, Judaism ✡, Hinduism ॐ and Sikhism ☬ it is almost an act of worship to look after the world. In all the religions, stewardship is a duty that God has set for humans. A 'duty' is a responsibility, a job – so looking after the world is one of the jobs humans have to undertake.

Future's thinking

What does this mean?

You can probably work it out – it is thinking about the future. We all do that, so let's work out why it is key for religious people.

◆ Firstly, if I trash my house, I have to live in the mess. So in terms of the world, whatever I do to it, I still have to live there.

◆ Secondly, others live there too, so they suffer. It's the same with the world – the damage I do affects others. In the future the things we do will affect our own children. And it's no good to say it wasn't us, it was our parents and grandparents, because the crisis point has been reached. Everybody has to help, whether or not they did anything to cause the problems.

◆ Thirdly, if I believe God made the world, and that I have a duty to look after it, then there must be a reward for doing my duty (or a punishment for not!), so it is in my interests to look after the world for God as God will reward me (heaven).

◆ Alternatively, I might be Buddhist, Hindu or Sikh. In these cases, I believe I will live on earth again after dying in this lifetime. So stewardship is still in my interests, as I need to come back!

The Basics

1 Match these words and phrases:
   Creation   Duty to look after the world
   Stewardship   Impact of problems in the future
   Future's thinking   Idea that God created the world from nothing
2 Find out a creation story from a religion and rewrite it. You could use images to retell it.
3 **Only religious people have a duty to look after the world**. What do you think? Explain your opinion.

Now you know some religious attitudes to the world

The earth and God – seeing God in nature

We really have to wonder why all these religions came up with the idea that God created the world.

Can you imagine the scene, many thousands of years ago, where a child asks his grandfather how all the world came to exist? Perhaps they are sitting around the fire, late in the evening, with a vast, star-filled sky above them. Imagine it – all is quiet except for the sounds of insects and animals, the fire crackles, the grandfather is telling stories from their people's history. The boy gazes at the world around him and the deep, inky blackness of the sky which is peppered with twinkling lights. It isn't difficult to imagine grandfather telling him the story of how the world was made by a great being – the greatest of all, because only such a being could create the world. The beauty and sense of peace can't all just be an accident – it must have deliberately been done. How did this being make it? Well, there wasn't anything to start with, because beginnings are always empty. Then you need a place, then the right conditions before you put life on it, from simple to complex. So, the boy is satisfied – and even more awe-struck by the world around him that he now sees in a different way.

> *Have you ever seen something in nature which has amazed you – maybe left you thinking 'wow'? Or something which made you go silent in awe?*

People see beautiful landscapes, sunsets, sunrises, waterfalls – these can make you feel privileged to have seen them, as if it was a special moment. That feeling is what we call 'awe'. The exam might ask you about 'awe and wonderment' – in other words things that make you feel amazed in the way just described.

So, it isn't hard to see why nature can inspire people to think of God. Also to see that nature provides a proof of God's existence for many people. We as simple humans must wonder at this power which is shown in the created world. If we wonder at it, we must respect the God who made it, and even worship that God by looking after the world.

The Basics

1 What is 'awe and wonderment'?
2 Why do you think some people see God in nature? Use some examples from nature to show what you mean.
3 Find some pictures of nature that help to show this sense of awe.

Research Task

The Alliance of Religions and Conservation (www.arcworld.org) has absolutely loads of stuff on this topic. Put a project or presentation together for the religion(s) you are studying. It will give you a better and clearer understanding of their attitudes and actions, which you can use in the exam.

Now you know how people are inspired by the world around them

World problems

1 Climate change and global warming

Climate change is what it says – that the climate is changing. Scientists tell us that their records show the earth is getting hotter. So temperatures everywhere will get higher – this is *global warming*.

Why is it happening?

It could be that the earth's cycle is to get hotter and cooler over time – you've heard of the ice ages, when the earth froze over, well this is the opposite. So this climate change and global warming is all part and parcel of the earth's life. However, scientists know that the activities of humans over the last 250 years, and especially the last 100, have speeded up temperature change. They estimate that the surface temperature of the earth will increase between 1.4 and 5.8°C before 2100. This is mainly because of the gases released by burning fossil fuels as energy or transport. Scientists are telling us we need to act now because if we are the problem, then we should be able to solve it.

So what are the consequences?

Imagine British summers being so hot that you don't need to go to Greece to get a tan! Sounds good? Hotter usually means dryer so plants and animals have to adapt or die. Hotter also means more frequent extreme weather. Hotter means some places become too hot to live in. The ice caps melt, so seas rise, so lands flood (and Britain isn't much above current sea-level!) If it gets too hot, diseases like malaria and dengue fever will come to Britain. Still sound great?

Solutions?

Scientists say the key solution is to change our energy use. We need to find alternatives to fossil fuels (coal, gas and oil) so that fuels either don't add to the problem, or are renewable. This is called *sustainable energy* – energy we can keep using without doing more harm.

The Basics

1 What is meant by 'climate change' and 'global warming'?
2 Why do scientists think the earth is getting hotter?
3 What is the main change we can make to try to slow this effect?
4 List as many forms of renewable energy as you can.
5 Imagine what school would be like if climate change happened. What problems would there be? What solutions can you come up with?
6 **A hotter world is a better world**. What do you think? Explain your opinion.

Now you know about climate change/global warming

Buddhist attitudes to the environment ☸

Buddhists believe that all life, in all forms, should be respected, that means the natural world. Since everyone must live many lifetimes, it is important to protect the world for our own future, as well as our children's. Two key beliefs for Buddhists are *respect* and *compassion*.

The Dalai Lama has said:

- **destruction** of nature and **natural resources** results from ignorance, greed, and lack of respect for the earth's living things…This lack of respect extends to future generations who will inherit a degraded planet
- the earth is not only the common heritage of all humankind but also the ultimate source of life
- conservation is not merely a question of morality, but a question of our own survival.

Buddhism also teaches:

- help not harm other sentient beings (First Precept)
- compassion for all life
- there are karmic consequences to all of our actions.

Looking after the environment isn't just about us – it's about the people of the future, it's about the other forms of life now and in the future. Ignorance and greed are two of the three poisons that keep people from enlightenment, and much environmental damage is because of people/ companies wanting more (money, space, whatever else) for themselves. Organisation website – www.earthsangha.org.

Christian attitudes to the environment ✝

Christians believe that God created the world and gave humankind stewardship – the responsibility to look after the world. Christians in modern times especially have seen the need to work to *heal the world*, and look after the environment.

Christianity teaches:

- God made the world, and gave the duty of stewardship to humans (Genesis).
- The earth is the Lord's, and everything in it (Psalms).
- Respect for life extends to the rest of creation (Pope John Paul II).
- More than ever, individually and collectively, people are responsible for the future of the planet (Pope John Paul II).
- I want to awake in you a deep admiration for creation, until anywhere thinking of plants and flowers, you are overcome by thoughts of the Creator (St Basil).

Clearly, Christians believe that humans have a special role on earth, which is to look after the earth and animals. Since humans must face God on the Day of Judgement, all must carry out their given duties. If humans did not look after the world, or did nothing to stop its destruction, they should expect to be punished by God. Many Christians are motivated to do environmental work because of this belief.

Organisation website – www.christian-ecology.org.uk.

2 Pollution

Pollution basically means there is too much of something, which has caused an imbalance and damage to the environment. It can be of air, water, or land. We even now talk about light and noise pollution. Usually, it is a result of what humans have done.

> Can you think of some examples of pollution?

> Go back through your list – what are the potential problems caused by each kind of pollution?

Busy roads cause air pollution. This affects our health, and drives some wildlife away. It also makes *acid rain*, so that when rain falls, it poisons the land and water, and damages buildings and structures.

Factories can cause water pollution by emptying waste into rivers, which poison the fish. Fertiliser running off farmers' fields can kill all the fish, as it makes the algae grow too fast, taking the oxygen from the water. This is just one form of *toxic chemical* – chemicals which can kill in big doses. Too much *pesticide* does more damage to the ecosystem than intended, and can change its whole balance.

You are probably a land polluter because of dropping litter. Doesn't just look bad, it also kills lots of wild animals who eat it, or get trapped in it.

In towns and cities, you see fewer stars than when you are in the countryside. The lights at ground level block out the stars – light pollution is affecting our appreciation of the beauty around us.

People who live near airport runways suffer from noise pollution. Even if it doesn't affect their hearing, it makes life unpleasant, and affects the value of their homes.

Pollution is a big part of the reason for the increasing temperature. Our waste produces the greenhouse gases that heat the Earth.

The Basics

1 What do we mean by 'pollution'?
2 Give three types of pollution.
3 How does our pollution help to cause global warming?
4 **Pollution can't be stopped.** Do you agree? Explain your opinion.

Now you know about pollution

3 Destruction of natural habitats

You have just read about pollution – pollution is one reason why **natural habitats** are being destroyed. For example, if a tanker spills oil into the sea, it wipes out life in that area, and degrades the land for many years. Check out the *Torrey Canyon* spill to get a better idea of this.

Another reason for the destruction of natural habits is deforestation, where huge areas of forest are cut down, for example, to create grazing land for cattle, or to create areas for building, mining and roads. The trees, of course, are the habitat for many species – so these species are affected, even dying out. Also, the trees convert the carbon dioxide into the oxygen we breathe, so they help in the fight against global warming. Shame we are cutting so many down!

Land is cleared in Borneo for palm oil plantations. Orang-utans lose their habitat, and are now an endangered species.

The rainforests also contain many plants that can be used as medicines, which are lost with deforestation. There are thought to be many species of animals and plants that we haven't even recorded yet in the rainforests – they could become extinct before we have even studied them.

Clearing land to build factories, for farming, and for people to live on also causes the destruction of natural habitats. When we clear the vegetation, we take away the home of some animals. We also destroy plants, sometimes putting the species into danger of extinction.

> *How could we make up for destroying these habitats?*

The Basics

1. What is 'destruction of natural habitat'? What does this lead to?
2. Give some reasons why this happens.
3. How could we avoid this destruction?
4. **God gave humans dominion over the world. This means we can do what we like.** What do you think? Explain your opinion.

Now you know about destruction of habitats

Hindu attitudes to the environment 🕉

Traditionally, Hindu life was very simple, and relied on the environment. This was linked with beliefs about the sanctity of life and non-violence to form a religion that is peaceful towards the environment. Brahman (the Ultimate Reality) is in all life.

Hinduism teaches:

- Respect for all life.
- Ahimsa – non-violence.
- Hindus should focus on environmental values (*Artharva Veda*).
- Trees have five sorts of kindness which are their daily sacrifice: to families they give fuel; to passers-by they give shade and a resting place; to birds they give shelter; with their leaves, roots and bark they give medicines (Varaha Purana).
- Everything rests on me as pearls are strung on a thread. I am the original fragrance of the earth...the taste in water...the heat in fire and the sound in space... the light of the sun and moon and the life of all that lives (Bhagavad Gita 7:7).

All life is seen as interdependent, including animals and plants. All life depends on the environment, so everyone needs to protect and look after it. Hindus believe all souls will be reborn into more lifetimes on earth, so we have to look after the earth for our own future sakes. God is seen as part of nature, so protection and worship are important.

Organisation website – www.fov.org.uk.

Muslim attitudes to the environment ☾

Islam sees the universe as the work of Allah. Humans are khalifah – stewards. Looking after the world shows respect to Allah.

Islam teaches:

- The world is green and beautiful, and Allah has appointed you his stewards over it (Qur'an).
- It has been created as a place of worship (Qur'an).
- When Doomsday comes, if someone has a palm shoot in his hand, he should still plant it (Hadith).
- The earth has been created for me as a mosque and a means of purification (Hadith).
- Prophet Muhammad (pbuh) gave the example of not wasting – he only washed in water from a container, not running water.

So, humans are the trustees of Allah's creation. Trustees look after things, not destroy them.

The creation reflects Allah. Allah knows who damages and who looks after his creation. Those who do not follow their duty to look after the world will be punished on Judgement Day.

The Muslim community is *Ummah*, (brotherhood), including those in the past and future. Everyone has a duty to make sure they pass on a world fit to live in, not one damaged beyond repair because humans were selfish.

Organisation website – www.ifees.org.

4 Use and abuse of natural resources

Natural resources include vegetation, minerals and fossil fuels. Humans are using these in greater quantities and at a faster rate now than at any other time in our history. This is because of how technologically advanced we are. We can cut materials out of the ground faster and in greater quantities than ever before. We use more fossil fuels at a faster and greater rate than ever before. Our technology, cars and all forms of transport, for example, needs more of them. More and more people in the world are getting more and more technology. We are also richer, so we use more resources. For example, more people go on holiday by plane, which uses much fuel.

Some of the fossil fuels, such as coal, are already running out. These fuels are limited in quantity and take millions of years to be formed. We either have to stop using them, or find a different source of energy, which is renewable. If we don't stop using them, and they run out, we will have to find a new source anyway.

What will be the problems caused if, for example, oil runs out?

It isn't just that these fuels are limited. They give off lots of the greenhouse gases, and cause the pollution which we have already mentioned. The more we use, the more the problems stack up. So finding an alternative helps us with those problems too – it isn't something we can hide from.

The Basics

1. What do we mean by 'use and abuse of natural resources'?
2. Give some examples of how we use natural resources.
3. Give some examples of our overuse, or abuse, of natural resources.
4. Why do we need to find new ways to get energy?
5. What new energy forms could there be?
6. **Ban the use of fossil fuels now.** What do you think? Explain your opinion.

✔ Now you know about use/abuse of natural resources

5 Modern living

Think about your life. What do you do to contribute to the problems we've read about in the last few pages?

It's really easy to think that global warming, pollution and so on are someone else's fault, and someone else's problem. It's also easy to think the problems are too big for us as individuals to do anything about. In our everyday lives, we put huge demands on the planet.

Can you give examples of some of the demands of everyday life?

How many of these questions do you answer 'no' to?

1 Does your family have a car or cars?
2 Does your family eat every scrap of food bought?
3 Do you only eat all-organic and free-range food?
4 Do you eat 'fast foods'?

Cars use up fossil fuels, and are a major polluter. The gases they put out (**emissions**) add to the greenhouse effect. If you buy more than you eat, there is **waste** in all kinds of ways – the food, its wrappings. Most food has been grown using pesticides, which will have polluted its local environment. Rain on the crops runs off, taking the pesticides with it into the soil or nearby water as a poison. Waste goes into landfill sites, which emit greenhouse gases as their contents decompose. The meat for fast-food burgers often comes from herds that graze cleared rainforest land, leading to the destruction of natural habitats.

So, you see, you are contributing to the problems we've read about. The question is – *what can you do about it?*

We could each take responsibility for our own contribution, and show respect to ourselves and the rest of the planet (now and in the future) by trying to solve the current problems. This is the message of governments and religions.

The Basics

1 Give two examples each of: emissions and waste.
2 How does the *demand* of modern living make the problems we have read about worse?
3 **People today only think of themselves, not the planet.** Think of reasons to agree and disagree.

Jewish attitudes to the environment ☰

Jewish sacred writings begin with G-d's creation of the world, and go on to state that G-d gave humans the duty of stewardship. There are many mitzvot (rules) about this.

Judaism teaches:

- All is made by G-d and is good. Humans are given stewardship over the creation (Genesis).
- The *Bal tashchit* (do not waste) precept can be read as an instruction to conserve resources (Torah).
- The earth and everything that is in it is the Lord's (Ketuvim).
- All that I created for you...do not corrupt or desolate my world...there will be no one to repair it after you (Midrash Ecclesiastes Rabbah 7 v 13).
- Love your neighbour as yourself (Leviticus).

So, Jews have a duty to look after the world, and should do this by treating it with respect. For example, land is to be left fallow on a regular cycle. Increasingly, Jews are becoming more active in environmental work, and are linking existing Jewish values to the issue. For example, tikkun olam (repairing the world) could be interpreted as tackling environmental problems; tzedek (justice) is extended to mean justice for all of creation, including animals and the world itself. It isn't possible to 'love your neighbour' if you are wrecking the environment!

Organisation website – www.coejl.org

Now you have thought about the demand of modern living

Sikh attitudes to the environment

For Sikhs the natural environment is a gift from God and we have to take care of it. It only exists because God wants it to. Sikhs believe the world is now in a 300-year cycle (Cycle of Creation), which gives a greater need to look after the world.

Sikhism teaches:

- The universe comes into being by God's will (**Guru Nanak**).
- In nature we see God, and in nature, we hear God speak (Adi Granth).
- Respect for all life.
- God created everything (Guru Nanak).
- The Sikh ideal is a simple life free from conspicuous waste.

Sikhs believe they must perform sewa (service) for others, which can include the natural world. Looking after the world safeguards it for future generations – sewa for people in the future. They believe that you can't care for the environment without thinking about society's needs, because often environmental damage is a result of **poverty**.

The gurdwaras in India have signed up to a plan to use solar power for their langars, which feed thousands every day. Sikh gurus said God is within everything, so in some ways damaging the world is like damaging God.

Visit www.arcworld.org/projects_overview.asp and follow the religion links to Sikhism.

Looking after the world
International efforts

Every ten years since 1972, there have been Earth Summits. Stockholm was the first. Governments of countries everywhere attend these summits, and discuss issues affecting the world. These issues are directly or indirectly about the environment. In 1972, the meeting discussed the global environment and development needs of the world. These two things conflicted. Immediately, the governments began to seek solutions. The Stockholm Declaration and Action Plan set out principles for helping the natural environment, and needing to support nations through this process.

In the 1980s, 'Our Common Future' recognised that humans needed to find ways to meet the needs of all people and countries today, whilst not messing things up for people in the future.

In 1992, at Rio de Janeiro, agreements were reached on Biodiversity and Climate Change. These led to the formation of the Commission for Sustainable Development. This said that we had to look for ways in which we could develop technologies which would keep going, for example, replacing fossil fuels with renewable energies.

Overall, these summits try to build agreements between nations. They try to help nations face the problems they have, whilst not heaping up problems for others or for the future. They try to stop the biggest nations from just doing their own thing at the expense of the smaller nations. They recognise that developing countries can't do the things that developed countries can – because they simply aren't rich enough. They try to encourage the sharing of the problems, and the solutions. Most of all, they are designed to put these issues on to the highest, most powerful agenda of the world leaders.

Kyoto agreements (2002 Summit)

In 2002, 83 governments plus the European Union signed up to these agreements. Countries signing up *agreed to set targets* for the future.

1 Cleaner fuels – use of gas, rather than fossil fuels; using fuel-cell technology; using renewable fuels, such as solar, wind and wave energies; and use of nuclear technologies.
2 Reducing the amount of carbon dioxide emissions.

The USA and Australia later withdrew from these agreements, feeling they were not in the interests of their nations. They have set up their own targets.

If countries can stick to these targets, then the results will have a positive impact on reducing global warming. If we can do that, the ice caps will melt less quickly, the life forms in those areas will be less endangered and perhaps even saved, the increasingly freak weather we have seen will be reduced, the deserts may stay where they are, and so on, and so on. It really is a big deal for the world to solve.

Learn about the problems in more detail — Recycle household waste — Campaign to make government change — Pray — Join an organisation, like Greenpeace — Go on an environmental action holiday — Pay for a tree to be planted — Use renewable energy — Don't waste stuff – buy only what you need — Grow a butterfly and bee garden — Walk don't drive — Eat organic — Be vegetarian — Encourage others to do the same

Sustainable development

This is the heart of the Earth Summits and all the agreements. It is the idea that new technological developments should all be infinite, or very long lasting, as well as within the reach of nations. It would be no use swapping coal as a fuel for something else which will quickly run out. Similarly, it would be no good finding a new technology that was simply too expensive for anyone to use.

Conservation

You must have heard the term **conservation.** It means when we try to protect an area or species. Sometimes it involves doing a whole load of repair and rebuild jobs somewhere, for example, to maintain the environment for an endangered species. It might include planting trees to protect an area from landslides. It might be declaring an area a nature reserve in order to protect wildlife and the environment there – this has happened in Borneo to protect orang-utans.

It is becoming more common for people to take holidays which are based around conservation – either of animals, like working on a lion reserve for a few weeks in Kenya, or environmental, like rebuilding dry stone walls in Scotland to protect vegetation in fields beyond these pathways.

Task

Find out about a conservation project that is going on near to you.

What about you – what can you do?

Check out the tape round the edge of this page – there are some ideas. Are there any you do already? Are there any you could do? Every little helps!

The Basics

1. What do we mean by 'international efforts' to save the planet?
2. Why do countries need to work together?
3. What are the Earth Summits, and what do they do?
4. Explain what we mean by 'sustainable development'.
5. Why are the Kyoto agreements important?
6. Explain, using examples, what we mean by 'conservation'.
7. List some of the things anyone can do to help the planet.

Exam Tips

For the exam, you need to be able to write about how all people, whether religious or not, can help the environment. The exam wants you to know about international efforts – what governments and big organisations are doing.

Now you know about solving the problems

Exam practice

How do you revise? Do you read page after page, and hope it soaks in? If you do, I've got bad news for you. That is one of the most inefficient ways to revise – sorry!

Would you like to be able to write everything about one topic on to one sheet? You can learn how here. Some people like to use this method at the start of their revision – an overview of what they have to learn. Others use it as a checklist at the end. I'd recommend both ways.

You will need – A3 paper, lots of different coloured pens, and your notes (just in case!).

Look at the chart on the next page – we'll call it a thought map.

In the centre, in big letters is the topic name. It needs to stand out, so you know what the page is about. Here, it is *PLANET EARTH*, it could be any topic you choose IN ANY SUBJECT (not just RE).

Around it at the first level are the chunks which make up that topic. These are the general issues that the exam questions will be based on, for example, questions about how we look after our world. Each chunk has its own colour. When you try to remember the bits of the chart, those colours will help your brain to organise the ideas.

Around each element are the relevant sections. They continue the colour of their element. These make up the foci of the questions, for example, saying we look after our world by conservation efforts.

You can add the details for each of those sections. They are what your answers will include. For example, issues to do with looking after our world might include – God created everything; stewardship means looking after it, and so on. Use the same colour for the rest of that bit of the chart.

This chart isn't finished, loads more can be added – try to do that for yourself.

Don't forget this though: the exam will want you to show that you *know the key words* and *what they mean*; it wants you to be able to give *examples* of them; to know why they are an issue/why they happened; and, it wants to see that you know *what the religions think*. Make sure you get all that on to your thought map.

Do this for any topic. Use a sheet of A3 sized paper. Stick it on your bedroom wall – you'll read it both deliberately and by accident there. What details you don't remember, check back in your notes. Add any that won't stick.

Happy revising!

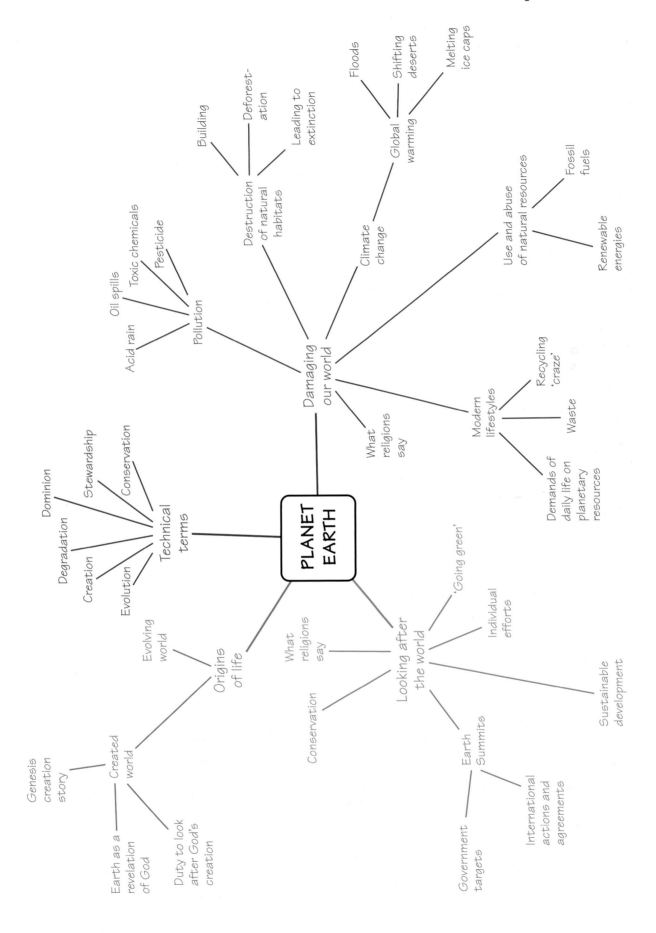

PLANET EARTH

Technical terms
- Dominion
- Stewardship
- Conservation
- Degradation
- Creation
- Evolution

Damaging our world
- Pollution
  - Oil spills
  - Toxic chemicals
  - Pesticide
  - Acid rain
- Destruction of natural habitats
  - Building
  - Deforestation
  - Leading to extinction
- Climate change
  - Global warming
    - Floods
    - Shifting deserts
    - Melting ice caps
- Use and abuse of natural resources
  - Fossil fuels
  - Renewable energies
- Modern lifestyles
  - Recycling 'craze'
  - Waste
  - Demands of daily life on planetary resources
- What religions say

Origins of life
- Evolving world
- Created world
  - Genesis creation story
  - Earth as a revelation of God
  - Duty to look after God's creation

What religions say

Looking after the world
- 'Going green'
- Individual efforts
- Sustainable development
- Conservation
- Earth Summits
  - Government targets
  - International actions and agreements

Topic Three Religion and prejudice

Definitions

The two key words for this topic are **prejudice** and **discrimination**. If you can learn what they mean, it will help with this whole topic. The two words are linked but their meaning is slightly different. Prejudice means to pre-judge something or someone, usually without any real evidence to base that judgement on. In most cases it is negative. We use the word to describe a person's dislike of certain other people, when they have no good reason. We talk about prejudice against colour, religion, age, nationality, sexuality or appearance. Prejudice is about what we *think*.

Discrimination is when we put these prejudiced ideas into action. We treat people differently or say things because they are not the same as us or what we know – we make known to them our dislike and it can have a great effect on a person's life. In Britain it is against the law to discriminate against someone. However, discrimination can be used *positively*, especially for minority groups and we will see some examples later on. Can you pick out the example of positive discrimination in the pictures opposite?

Rugby is a man's sport.

We don't want any white girls in our gang.

So, what do you need to know?

You need to learn the words above, and then investigate how it all happens. It's important to know – what causes people to act in this way or even think ideas like this in the first place; what effect these actions can have; different types of discrimination; what religion(s) think about these actions and how they respond when discrimination happens; what the law says about discrimination; and finally, what some famous individuals have done to prevent and fight discrimination.

In order to bring all the areas of discrimination together, it will be useful for you to keep four key ideas in your mind.

POLICE/FIRE SERVICE

VACANCIES
Black or Gay officers

Tolerance – to accept that people have different opinions and beliefs from your own.
Justice – that everyone has the same rights and deserves the same treatment.
Community and **Harmony** – a collection of people (a community) who live and work together to help each other so that everyone benefits. The community accepts each member – including their differences (harmony).

I'm a Muslim.

I'm a Jew, but we can still be friends.

EQUAL PAY!
That's only fair!

Come on, we need to do this together.

Let's look a little deeper

What makes someone prejudiced and want to discriminate against others?

It is true to say that everyone can be prejudiced at times, even by accident. Not everyone will discriminate against others though because of their prejudice. Which is the more serious – the thought or the action? It is an interesting question to think about!

> *Think about this – because it's a popular exam question.*

Bad experience

Parents/upbringing

Media

Ignorance

Scapegoating

Prejudice can be like a brick wall – a barrier that stops people living, working and learning together as a community. It is very unfair and it only takes someone to be 'different' to be singled out for discrimination. The victims are almost always in the minority and find it very hard to deal with.

Anyway, there are five main reasons for prejudice:

1 Having a *bad experience* with someone might make you think everybody is like that. For example, maybe when you were young you were frightened by a grumpy old man and now you think all old men are grumpy.

2 Having been told bad things about a certain group of people by your *parents,* you might be prejudiced without even getting a chance to know any differently. Our upbringing has a big influence on us, and our parents' words have a huge effect.

3 Having seen something on television or read it in a newspaper (or other forms of *media*) that was very biased (it focused on only one fact or idea, taking it out of context), you might have believed it and so now are prejudiced.

4 When you've gone ahead and judged someone when you actually know nothing about them. This is called *ignorance.* For example, having a negative opinion about a group of people, whom you have never met or actually learned anything about – you don't know them, but you insult them anyway.

5 *Scapegoating* is when you blame or use others as an excuse for a problem. For example, Hitler blamed the Jews for the economic problems in Germany. He used the media and speeches to influence the German people so much that they also blamed the Jews, which cleared the way for the Holocaust. In actual fact, the Jewish people in Germany had done nothing wrong.

The Basics

1 What is meant by 'prejudice' and 'discrimination'?
2 Explain how the top three pictures on page 30 are examples of discrimination.
3 Give some examples of your own of discrimination.
4 Why is 'tolerance' important in helping to prevent prejudice?
5 Explain some reasons why some people might be prejudiced.
6 Choose three of these reasons and give an example to demonstrate each one. Choose different examples to the ones shown on page 30.
7 **You need to change the way people think to prevent discrimination.** What do you think? Explain your opinion.

Can we challenge these ideas?

Let's look at some commonly used discriminative statements from the variety of people below:

I think women should stay at home so when I get married I won't let my wife work.

Adam

I think young people these days are all layabouts so I won't have them working in my firm.

George

I saw two men holding hands, it's unnatural, so I thumped one of them when they walked past.

Andrea

Me and my mate nicked this guy's prayer hat 'cos religion is a joke.

Richie

I think fashions like Goths are horrible and I tell them that when I see them all dressed in black.

Reeta

I was in McDonald's the other day and this fat woman sat at my table so I got up and walked out.

Suki

Task 1

In pairs, for each of the examples shown in the illustrations, work out:

a   What type of prejudice is being shown.
b   What was done to show discrimination.
c   What you would say to challenge each of these people.

Task 2: Snowballing exercise

Students should be in groups of four or five. Each group needs a large sheet of paper or a writing board.

In your life you must have experienced or seen discrimination happen or watched examples of it on television. In the centre of your sheet/board example write down the one your group chooses to focus on.

The sheet/board should now be passed in turn to each group for them to add a statement to challenge the example or what it describes, such as saying why the action is wrong and what could be done to deal with the situation.

Each group is given a few minutes to add to the new sheet in front of them. It is often the case that we can learn from others and sometimes what someone else says/writes can spark ideas of our own.

Try it for another task and see for yourself!

Positive discrimination

After looking at all this negative stuff you must remember that discrimination can also be positive. In some cases benefits can be given to people in minority groups to give them greater chances. For example, over the last ten years the police and fire services have actually advertised for people in minority groups to apply for jobs. This would give an advantage to people from ethnic minorities, women or gay/lesbian groups – people who are often the victims of discrimination. The reason behind this was to try and make these services more representative of the society we live in today. Of course, positive discrimination can help in challenging prejudice.

Now you know how discrimination can be challenged

Can you think of any other ways we can discriminate positively?

Types of prejudice

On the following pages you will see that the religious teachings are general and can be applied to all forms of prejudice. *Only focus on the religion(s) that you are studying.* Think about how each teaching/religious idea can be applied to each of the forms of prejudice. Remember – *tolerance, justice, community* and *harmony*.

Ageism

This is discrimination against someone because of their age. Remember it can apply to anyone in any age group.

When the law sets age limits (for example an age to drive, smoke or drink), it is not seen as ageist. These limits are for our own good.

Look at the elderly first – we might expect them to not be fit enough for a job, or too old to understand modern ways. This leads them to be undervalued by society. With the young, it might be a case of thinking they're too young to take on some kind of responsibility.

All religions believe in respecting the elderly – they teach that everyone is equal. Older people are wiser, therefore they should be listened to. It is a duty of the young to look after them. The young are the future and quite often children become 'adults' in their own religion at an early age. Old or young, the value of the individual is very important.

Sexism

Sexism is prejudice because of someone's gender. We often see examples against women. Many religions see men's and women's roles as different, but still equal. They do not agree with prejudice and discrimination against either gender – it is unfair and therefore wrong.

A woman serving in the army

There are a growing number of female teams in previously male-dominated sports like rugby

Religious teachings

Buddhism

Buddhism believes that as discrimination leads to suffering then it must be wrong and should be avoided.

- The belief not to harm others or use harmful language (Five Precepts).
- Everyone should try to develop *metta* (loving kindness).
- Everyone is equal because everyone is welcome in the Sangha.
- Prejudice creates bad karma and has a negative effect on rebirth.
- The Dalai Lama stated that the best way to live life was to 'Always think compassion'.

Christianity

Christianity believes that all forms of discrimination are wrong.

- God created everyone equally (Old Testament).
- 'There is neither Jew nor Gentile, slave or free man, male or female. We are all equal in Christ' (New Testament).
- 'So in everything, do unto others what you would have done to you' (New Testament).
- Jesus told us to love our neighbour (Sermon on the Mount).
- In the Good Samaritan story the man is helped because of his need, not because of who he was or wasn't (New Testament).

The role of women in religions

Within religion there is a debate about the role of women. They are treated differently to men and there is often the accusation that women are being discriminated against despite the fact that all religions condemn any kind of discrimination. Let's look at some examples:

◆ In Christianity, women cannot be priests in the Roman Catholic Church or bishops in the Anglican Church.
◆ In Islam, all religious leaders are men and women don't pray at the front of the mosque.
◆ In Othodox Judaism, women sit separately to men, often upstairs, and do not take part in synagogue services.
◆ With the exception of ISKCON, in Hinduism all Brahmin priests are male.
◆ In Theravada Buddhism, women will pray for their reincarnation to be as a man.

If women are denied access to certain roles, then this could be said to be discriminatory. However, these religions would just say that roles are different but equal. If women are happy with their roles and what they are or are not permitted to do, then to them discrimination is not an issue. The issue arises when women want to do something as part of their religion but are not allowed to because rules or traditions say they can't.

As time moves on there are changes being made to traditions, but women have to fight hard for those changes. They would argue that if we are all creations of God, then if, for example, a woman wants to devote herself to the service of God and serve the community of believers, would God not want her to simply because she is a woman? Perhaps a woman could deal with community issues and help people in a different way to a man? Compassion and understanding are key qualities and many women have these.

It all depends on how you view this issue. It isn't the same as other forms of prejudice where people inflict hurt and pain on others. However, if you desperately want to do something or be part of something and cannot simply because of your gender, then for that woman it could be really hurtful.

Roman Catholic priests cannot be women

Most Hindu brahmin are men

There are no female imams in Islam

The Basics

1 What is meant by the words 'ageism' and 'sexism'?
2 Explain religious teaching about sexism.
3 Give some examples of ageist behaviour.
4 **Women should be allowed to be leaders in religion.** Explain two reasons to agree, and two to disagree.

So now you know about ageism and sexism

Disability

ParalympicsGB

Eleanor Simmonds won two swimming gold medals at the 2008 Paralympics. She shattered the British record and beat the world record holder. She is an inspiration to all and shows that we all have talents.

Quite often people who have a **disability** are discriminated against. A disability includes two key areas: physical disabilities such as wearing glasses, being in a wheelchair, not having a limb; and mental disabilities such as having a learning problem or a mental illness.

Could a person in a wheelchair access your school? How often do we talk to the person pushing the wheelchair not the person in it? Have you witnessed someone call a person who is hearing or sight impaired names? It is as if they are less of a person than someone fully able-bodied. Religion believes that all people are equal and God creates people in many different ways. We are all valued despite our differences. The example at the top of the page clearly shows that people overcome difficulties and can reach the highest possible achievements.

Looks and lifestyle

The way people look is often the first thing that incites prejudiced thoughts – the clothes people wear, hair style or colour, tall or short, fat or thin. On first meeting a stranger these things might be enough for us to instantly decide whether we like them or not. For some, these first impressions stick and they don't give people a chance. This in turn leads to discriminatory comments or actions. We could think of Sophie Lancaster in Lancashire who, in 2007, was murdered because she was a Goth. She chose to be different and as a result this led to discrimination of the worst kind – she lost her life! Likewise if people choose to live a different way to us or to what we accept to be 'normal' – such as people who live together (rather than marry), gay couples or travellers – then this often leads to discrimination. Religion would not agree with any discriminatory actions. It may be true that the religion does not agree with the choices people make, particularly with regards to lifestyle, but it would totally disagree with showing discrimination in such cases.

The Basics

1 **Discrimination is the worst thing a person can suffer.** What do you think? Explain your opinion.
2 **Being discriminated against because of a disability is worse than sexism.** Do you agree? Give reasons and explain your answer, showing you have thought about more than one point of view. Refer to religious arguments in your answer.

Hinduism ॐ

Hindu Dharma (teaching) is that Brahman is found in everything, therefore any prejudice thoughts or discriminative actions would be viewed as wrong.

- Hindus believe in non-violence (ahimsa), love and respect for all things.
- Compassion is a key belief with the desire to improve things for others, not persecute them.
- Hurting others can lead to bad karma, which affects future reincarnations.
- Hindus believe that the true self is the **atman** and as everyone has one this must mean everyone is equal.
- The Bhagavad Gita suggests that to reach liberation you should work for the welfare of all fellow human beings.

Islam ☪

Islam teaches that Allah created everyone as equal but different.

- This was Allah's design, so discrimination is unjustified (Qur'an).
- Allah loves the fair minded (Qur'an).
- The Five Pillars (beliefs and actions) apply to all people equally.
- Muhammad (pbuh) allowed a black African man to do the call to prayer in Madinah and he welcomed anyone regardless of wealth, status or creed.
- The Muslim Declaration of Human Rights states that everyone is equal.
- On Hajj (the greatest Muslim gathering on earth), everyone is equal in dress and action.

Now you know why prejudice might happen

Racism

Racism is the belief that the colour of a person's skin, or their race, affects their ability. It is also the belief that some races are better than others. We use the word 'racist' to describe someone who

discriminates against people of other races in a negative way. The slave trade was based on the belief that people of colour were somehow of less value than other people, and so could be bought and sold and treated in any way with no rights at all. It cost the lives of countless tens of thousands, and destroyed many communities. The attitude of superiority it created still exists in the world today. Look at the statistics in the UK – if you are black, you are more likely to get excluded from school, to achieve less highly than others, to get stopped by the police more often, to get sent to prison, to be murdered – it goes on. Our society needs to change, and racism needs to be ended.

Racism is illegal. We'll see the Race Relations Act details a bit later. Most people think racism is wrong. Why should a person's skin colour or race make a difference? It shouldn't. If you are actively racist, you can pay a heavy price. You could lose your job, get thrown out of school, go to prison…

'All human beings are born free and equal…should act in a spirit of brotherhood…everyone is entitled to all the rights and freedom' (*Universal Declaration of Human Rights*).

Religious prejudice

Many people today face prejudice because of their religion. This has always happened over history because religions mark people out. Often religious people wear symbols of their religion, which makes them easy to spot. They have beliefs that shape their behaviour. When these religions are a minority in a community they stand out, therefore becoming a target for discrimination. For example, the Muslim community in non-Muslim countries after 9/11.

At the same time, religious communities can be guilty of discrimination against other minority religious groups in their own countries. For example in the Balkan Conflict, Serb forces (Catholic) were guilty of the ethnic cleansing of Muslim villages – they killed these people simply because they were Muslim.

Judaism ♆

Judaism teaches that prejudice and discrimination are incompatible with Jewish Law. Over the years, Judaism has been the target of disrimination to the extreme, and therefore Jews have strong opinions on the issue.

- G-d created everyone equal. So prejudice is seen as an insult to G-d.
- The Torah tells Jews to welcome and not persecute strangers.
- The Nevi'im states that G-d expects people to practise justice, love and kindness to all.
- Treat others as you wish to be treated (Torah).
- Jewish leaders state that Jews should live in harmony with non-Jews.

Sikhism ☬

Sikhism believes in the principle of justice and to fight for justice where it does not exist. Equality and sewa (service to others) would clearly indicate that discrimination is wrong.

- 'Using the same mud, the Creator has created many shapes in many ways' (Guru Granth Sahib).
- Those who love God love everyone (Adi Granth).
- God created everyone so all are equal and deserve the same treatment and respect (Mool Mantra).
- The use of the langar suggests everyone is welcome – Sikh or not.
- 'God is without caste' (Guru Gobind Singh).

Now you know about racism and religious prejudice

Homophobia

This is prejudice against people who are attracted to those of the same gender as themselves. Homosexuals and lesbians can face lots of prejudice (called homophobia) and are discriminated against because people do not agree with their relationships. Victims of other kinds of discrimination will often receive help from friends and family who sometimes face that same discrimination. However, for lesbians and homosexuals sometimes their families don't even know, or they even discriminate too. It can be very difficult, especially for young people who work out they may be gay and only have their families to turn to or possibly no one. Religions have differing opinions on the subject of homosexuality, but what they do agree with is that the discrimination of such people is wrong.

Lindsay Lohan and her girlfriend

George Michael

A gay couple on a Gay Pride march

Ellen DeGeneres and Portia de Rossi

Religious attitudes to homosexuality

The approach to homosexuality is slightly different from that of the other forms of prejudice we have looked at so far. Religions accept without question someone's age, race, or gender, for example; however, they usually don't agree with homosexuality. This means that even though they don't persecute homosexuals, they don't necessarily welcome them either. Some people think that sex between two men or two women is unnatural, and wrong. This is usually because it is impossible for this kind of sex to lead to children. From most religious viewpoints the primary reason for sex is the conception of children. It is also the case that in the holy books you can read quotes against homosexuality. In Britain, things are changing, same sex couples can legally register as couples. Religions emphasise this isn't the same as getting married, but does mean that under law they are protected. For example, they can get pension and inheritance rights, and other rights which married couples get automatically.

The Basics

1   What is meant by 'racism'?
2   Using examples, explain 'religious prejudice'.
3   Explain what is meant by 'homophobia'.
4   What are religious attitudes to homosexuality?

Now you know about homophobia

The effects of discrimination

Can you work out the emotions that these people are feeling due to having been discriminated against?

'I'm determined to beat this – it's been the same all my life – everyone having a go at me just because I'm gay. I will not let it stop me doing what I want or getting the job I want.'

'When I joined my new school after moving house it was hard to fit in because everyone knew each other. They called me names or smirked at me because of my accent. This upset me a lot.'

'I went for a job – I was by far the most qualified but my skin was obviously the wrong colour. I could have done the job with my eyes shut!'

The effects of discrimination

'I can't cope with this any more – day after day of bullying. There is this gang of girls who make my life a misery. I'm black and it's always about my colour – how I don't belong here and should go back to my own country. Sometimes it gets physical too. There is no other way out.'

'I'm a Muslim – my family is the only Muslim one in this area. Since 9/11 I've lost a lot of friends. No one talks to me and they treat me with suspicion. I've no one – my religion is important to me but so are people. It's hard to exist on your own.'

'I have decided that they are not going to get the better of me – I choose to dress this way; I like it and if they don't – tough! I won't let them get to me. I am all the more determined to wear what I want.'

These are all emotional effects from the individuals' perspective. When this multiplies to people in greater numbers and becomes the norm, then it can have a devastating effect on whole minority groups.

Ways religion can help the victims of discrimination

Religion can provide both practical and spiritual support to victims of discrimination. A religious book may have teachings that, when read, offer comfort and support and put things into perspective. Religious leaders can offer help and just be there to listen. They can organise meetings to highlight the problems or set up support groups. They can use school assemblies to promote tolerance and harmony.

On a spiritual level, they can pray with you or for you and if belief is strong enough, this can make you feel that you are not on your own.

Exam Tips

Remember the ways to help can be used in any question that asks you how religion can help someone suffering with any problem. You simply have to adapt them to the topic. It's less to revise, folks!

  Now you know about how religions try to fight prejudice

What the law says in Britain

The Fawcett Society traces its roots back to 1866, when the suffragette Millicent Garrett Fawcett began her lifetime's work leading the peaceful campaign for women's votes. It is the UK's leading organisation campaigning for equality between men and women.

The Fawcett Society campaigns on women's representation in politics and public life; pay, pensions and poverty; valuing caring work and the treatment of women in the justice system. It also produces research and reports and uses the media to raise awareness of inequality issues.

Check it out for yourself at www.fawcettsociety.org.uk.

Football Against Racism in Europe (FARE) is an organisation which spans Europe, using football as a common platform, trying to get rid of racism. The English link to this is Kickitout (www.kickitout.org), and their Show Racism the Red Card campaigns. FARE was set up in 1999, to bring together all the existing organisations in a Europe-wide network. It links the organisations, and sets up campaigns which span several countries. It has involved lots of the top footballers in each country to be a part of its work. Through activities such as tournaments, anti-racist matches, flyers at games, anti-racist T-shirts, and much more, it aims to rid football of racism. It also tries to promote racial harmony by helping mixed groups within football.

Check it out for yourself at www.farenet.org.

Stonewall is an organisation working for equality and justice for lesbians and gay men. It works on a political and social level throughout the UK. It is involved in many different campaigns, such as one in education called Education for All.

Check this out for yourself at www.stonewall.org.uk.

Age Concern is the UK's largest organisation working for and with older people. In England, they are a federation of over 400 charities working together to promote the well-being of all older people.

Age Concern's work ranges from providing vital local services to influencing public opinion and government. Every day they are in touch with thousands of older people from all kinds of backgrounds – enabling them to make more of life.

There are laws in Britain to deal with discrimination. As prejudice is about the way people think, the law cannot do anything, but when that prejudice turns into discriminative actions then the law can act. However, it is not always easy to prove.

The 1976 Race Relations Act (RRA) made it illegal to discriminate against anyone because of race, nationality, ethnic or national background in four main areas – jobs, education, housing and the provision of services. It made illegal the use of threatening or abusive language in regard to race. It also made it illegal to publish anything to stir up racial hatred.

The Commission for Racial Equality was set up to deal with cases of discrimination, and to act as a watchdog against racism. In 2000 the RRA Amendment Act was introduced as a way of strengthening the 1976 Act. It focuses on helping and protecting people in the public sector, the police service, areas of government and areas of national security. It also stresses the need to promote harmony and tolerance amongst all people.

There have also been laws passed about Equal Pay (1975), Sex Discrimination (1975), Disability Discrimination (1995) and the Sexual Orientation Regulation (2007).

As well as the law, there are organisations that support victims and try to improve awareness of the discrimination certain groups face.

Task

In groups, decide on a group in society that faces prejudice and discrimination. You are going to set up an organisation to work for the rights of this chosen group. Complete the following:

1 Design a logo for your organisation.
2 Write a mission statement to explain what you are about.
3 Produce a one-page leaflet to hand out to people at a meeting/rally your organisation is holding in the town centre.
4 Write a short persuasive speech to be used at this meeting/rally explaining why this particular discrimination is wrong.

Famous people – fighting to end prejudice and discrimination

Martin Luther King

Who was he?

Martin Luther King was born in the USA in 1929. As a black American, he soon realised the prejudice that black people faced simply because of their colour of skin. Black people were *segregated* – meaning they had separate schools, transport systems, shops, even churches. King was brought up in a Christian family and had a good education. He learned from his religion that colour shouldn't matter and his thinking was influenced by the Indian leader Mahatma Gandhi who fought for justice in a non-violent way. King is most famous for a speech he made beginning 'I have a dream...' The essence of this speech was his belief that everyone was equal and that people should be judged not by the colour of their skin but by the content of their character. Whilst he had great support, he also had enemies. In 1968 he was murdered. His death had great significance and indeed sparked even more people to campaign for equal rights.

Martin Luther King

What did he do to fight racism?

This is often the focus of exam questions – rather than asking about King's general life, what is being asked about are the ways in which he protested. So let's have a look.

The Civil Rights March on Washington, led by Martin Luther King

In 1955, King organised a bus boycott to try to end segregation on the buses. It took a year to achieve but, by the end, blacks could sit next to whites rather than sitting only at the back or standing up for a fellow white passenger. In 1957, King continued to preach non-violent direct action involving marches, boycotts and sit-ins. He marched with school children in 1963 to demonstrate about the poor education and schools that black children had. He continued to make political speeches at rallies and even the US President seemed to support his ideas. His fame spread worldwide. Things were starting to change – King said 'When I die my work will only just be beginning'.

So what was his legacy?

The years since King's death in 1968 have seen great change in the USA. Life is much improved for the black community. Segregation is illegal. Black people have equal civil rights with whites. However, things are not perfect and there is still a lot of poverty in many, mainly black areas. America has seen the emergence of black political leaders, Jesse Jackson in the 1970s and in November 2008 Barack Obama was elected as the next President of the USA. At the time of Martin Luther King's death, the idea of a black person running what is often considered to be the most powerful country in the world would have been unthinkable. Now King's dream has been realised.

Barack Obama

Martin Luther King Day is a national holiday in the USA around 20 January each year.

Archbishop Desmond Tutu

Who is he?

Archbishop Desmond Tutu receiving the Nobel Peace Prize

As his title tells you, Desmond Tutu is a religious leader. He was born in South Africa in 1931, a country where people lived under the Government Apartheid system. This was the total separation of the black and white community, with the minority whites in complete control of the country. As Desmond Tutu moved up the religious hierarchy, he began to use his position to campaign against the way the black community was treated. He took a great risk doing that because Apartheid was a government policy and if you criticised it, you faced torture and imprisonment. By 1976 he was already a bishop, and perhaps that gave him some sort of protection. He was known worldwide, and South Africa would have had lots of unwelcome and unfriendly attention if its government had done anything to him. In 1984 he was awarded the Nobel Peace Prize for his work. In 1986 he became Archbishop of Cape Town. Even today, at his old age, he still works both within his religion and politically.

What did he do?

His vision was for a totally non-racial South Africa where everyone mattered because they were all humans made in the image of God. He organised a non-violent struggle using marches, boycotts, petitions, and invited the international media into South Africa to show to the world what his people were suffering. This gave the issue world attention and brought international pressure on the South African white government to alter the Apartheid Laws.

An anti-Apartheid rally

So what has he achieved so far?

Things have changed in South Africa. The Apartheid system was dismantled, elections were held which resulted in a black President: Nelson Mandela. Currently South Africa has a black leader. Tutu still speaks out for the rights of the poorest groups and in his book, *Voice of One Crying in the Wilderness*, he calls for action to bring social justice to South Africa, and to other African countries. For the black majority, there are still massive improvements in standards of living to be made.

See www.tutu.org for more information.

A shanty town in South Africa

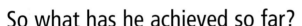

Task

Focus on both Martin Luther King and Desmond Tutu. Make a revision list of four facts about each of their lives, four things they did to achieve their goals and two ideas for each to say what they achieved. This will give you more than enough detail for your exam if you are asked to talk about someone famous who has fought against prejudice. It might be a surprise to you to find out how little you need to learn! Usually questions about individuals are worth 3–4 marks and, as such, this is enough detail for you to learn.

Mohandas K. Gandhi

Who was he?

Gandhi is known by the name 'Mahatma', which means great soul. He was born in India in 1869 when India was part of the British Empire, and led the Indian nationalist movement against British rule. His belief in non-violent protest to achieve his aims has influenced many other leaders around the world. He studied as a barrister, and in 1893 went to South Africa, where he worked to gain Indian migrants basic rights. They were discriminated against, but in 1914 the South African government accepted many of his demands for the Indian people, thanks, at least partly, to his work.

Gandhi

On his return to India, Gandhi got involved in protests against British rule. He carried out peaceful non-cooperation with the British including boycotts and marches. In 1930 he led a Salt Tax March because it was illegal for Indians to produce their own salt. He even went on hunger strike. He also focused his attention on the growing unrest between the Hindu and Muslim communities, trying to improve relations

Gandhi

between the two sides. Whilst much of his work was not directly to do with prejudice, what he wanted was an integrated society where everyone lived in harmony. He felt the structure of society would have to change if people were to have a better chance in life. He saw British policy as unfair on the Indian people. Although he was a Hindu, he didn't like the caste system. The lowest caste was known as 'the untouchables', yet Gandhi saw them as 'children of God' just like the rest of the human race. He fought to change attitudes to these people.

In 1947 British rule ended and India was split up (partitioned) along religious lines and the state of Pakistan was created. Mass violence was one of the results. Gandhi had objected to Partition, saying it would be disastrous. In 1948 he was assassinated.

So why was Gandhi such an important figure?

Gandhi left a great legacy of non-violence – his values and methods were taken up in many other struggles. He famously said 'An eye for an eye...and soon we shall all be blind' to show that violence was not the answer. Likewise, Desmond Tutu said 'You cannot use methods that our enemies will use against us'. Martin Luther King said 'You should meet hate with love'. All three men share the same values of peace and compassion – Tutu and King gaining their inspiration from Gandhi.

The Basics

1   Write down three things about Gandhi's life.
2   What methods did Gandhi use to achieve his aims?
3   What did Gandhi do in South Africa?
4   Explain what Gandhi did to improve the life of people in India.
5   **Without Gandhi, violence would always have been the main method of protest.** What do you think? Explain your answer.

Research Task

See www.bbc.co.uk/religion to find out more details about these people. You could build a presentation about them for others to learn from.

Exam tips – the ladder to success

This page contains a number of ideas that you could try, and which would help you to revise.

Revision tip 1
Lots of religions share the same key terms or ideas. Learn these terms and use them regularly in your exam. If you can only remember the list, you will still get about half the available marks. For example, religious beliefs about prejudice always come down to life being sacred, respect for God's creation, justice for all, and the equality of all. These ideas cross religions and topics of course.

Revision tip 2
Make a set of flashcards, and get someone to test your knowledge regularly with them. Put images and words on to the cards, such as examples of prejudice to name, or words to define, or religious ideas to link to prejudice. Someone holds up a flashcard, and you talk about it.

Revision tip 3
Collect pictures of as many of the things you study as you can. A picture with a caption sticks better in many people's heads than just writing. Then you can think of the image in the exams and it will help you remember, for example, pictures of people fighting prejudice with key words around the person.

Revision tip 4
Ballpark marking. After you've done a test and before it is marked, ask your teacher to tell you exactly what the marks were for in each question, and judge your answers from that. Compare your guesstimate with your real mark when you get your marked paper back. This makes you analyse your work more than you would if you just got it back marked. This means you understand better where you went wrong and how to improve.

Revision tip 5
Create an A4 sized thought map with the key issues this topic has covered. See page 29 for an example. If you do this for each full topic you will end up with six pages to learn for the final exam. Psychologically this is good because it means that you are not faced with endless pages of notes to learn. Your full notes are a reference to check fine detail. When it is done, try a five-minute focus on the diagram, then see how much you can reproduce – on average 75 per cent of it.

Revision tip 6
Timed tests are good for improving your timing. Here's a set of questions. Give yourself 25 minutes (with no books!)
1. Explain how religious believers have fought against prejudice and discrimination. (3 marks)
2. What do religions teach about prejudice and discrimination? (6 marks)
3. Discrimination is worse than prejudice. What do you think? Explain your opinion. (3 marks)
4. Some religious people have argued that it is not always wrong to discriminate against other people; it depends on the circumstances. Do you agree? Give reasons and explain your answer, showing you have thought about more than one point of view. (6 marks)

Exam practice

AO2 questions – examiner's tips

These are evaluative questions, and each full question will include two of these – one worth 3 marks and the other worth 6 marks. You have to do well on them, because they make up 50 per cent of the total mark. Let's check them out...

Evaluative questions always ask you what you think about something, or whether you agree. Actually, the exam isn't interested in whether or not you agree – it wants to know your reasoning. As long as you explain your reasons clearly, and you discuss the statement you were set, you should get marks.

3-mark AO2s

These start with a statement, then say *What do you think? Explain your opinion.* The examiner is interested in your opinion – as long as it relates to the statement. You will get marks for making a couple of points, and then explaining them, perhaps with an example to strengthen your argument. The exam watchdog (called QCA) wants to see opportunities for you to give personal insights, and this is where you do that. Let's try a couple...

1 **Religious prejudice is the worst kind of prejudice.** What do you think? Explain your opinion.

2 **Religious people should never discriminate.** What do you think? Explain your answer.

Getting used to the techniques of how to answer different types of questions effectively is really important as well. Quite often good technique means you can answer more clearly, and in a snappier style – this makes it easier for the examiner to give you better marks!

6-mark AO2s

Okay, for these you've got to do a whole lot more work. For a start, you will have to have religious arguments in there – you'll only get 3 marks max if you don't. Somewhere in the question there will be a prompt to remind you. Then, you have to answer from two sides, in other words you have to agree and disagree, each time explaining your ideas – 4 marks max if you don't.

Level	Description	Mark
0	Unsupported opinion or no relevant evaluation	0
1	Opinion (e.g. I agree) supported by one simple reason	1
2	Opinion supported by two simple reasons, or one elaborated reason	2
3	Opinion supported by one well-developed reason, or a series of simple reasons, on one or both sides.	3

Level	Description	Mark
4	Opinion supported by two developed reasons, with reference to religion	4
5	Evidence of reasoned consideration of two different points of view, with reference to religion	5
6	A well-argued response, with evidence of reasoned consideration of two different points of view and clear reference to religion	6

So let's build from the 3-marker, because the first levels for these questions are the same.

Let's try some more...

3 **Religions cause prejudice, rather than solve it.** Do you agree? Give reasons for your answer, showing you have thought about more than one point of view.

4 **Discrimination is worse than prejudice.** Do you agree? Give reasons for your answer, showing you have thought about more than one point of view. Refer to religious arguments in your answer.

'Developed' means you said something, and then explained it a bit.

'Reasoned consideration' just means some reasons with explanations.

This topic is essentially about the issue of **abortion**. Some women have abortions. They are operations/procedures to end pregnancy, and the intention is that the foetus does not live to be born. The topic wants you to look more deeply into this subject. It wants you to consider when life begins; what the law says; why some women request abortions; whose **rights** are the most important in the decision to abort; the arguments used by **Pro-Choice** and **Pro-Life** campaigners; and, of course, what the religion(s) think.

In the beginning...

When exactly does life begin?

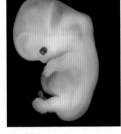

Is it at conception?

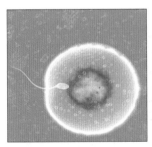

Is it when the foetus has a heart of its own, which beats?

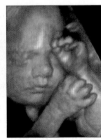

Is it when there is a backbone?

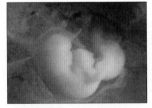

Is it when the foetus is likely to survive if born early?

Is it when it has been born?

This is a key question because many people see abortion as murder or killing, and there has to be a life before there can be a murder. It does affect whether or not we see an abortion as wrong.

By law, the life begins when the baby is born. The **Abortion Act** will not allow abortions beyond 24 weeks (less than 5 per cent of babies born in weeks 22 and 23 survive, even with the help of extended intensive care, and many of those go on to have many health problems at least in early life), so is that when life begins? Many people think that when the foetus looks like a baby, it should be treated as such – whether it is fully formed or not.

What we can say is that at every stage the foetus is a *potential life*.

Difficult question, then...

The Basics

Write out the different points at which people say life begins. For each one, say whether or not you agree and explain why. Sum up by restating when you believe life begins.

Research Task

The Education for Choice organisation has a very good website that covers all the arguments about abortion and is designed to help young people, especially, make informed choices about their sexual health. Check it out, and use it to boost your notes whilst you work on this topic. See www.efc.org.uk.

Now you have thought about when life begins

About children

When a couple marry, almost inevitably at some point they think about having children. Religious people are no different to anyone else, and most will have children within their marriage.

> *Why do you think people decide to have children?*

You probably came up with several main reasons such as, to show of their love for each other; to continue the family name; to fulfil a religious duty.

For most religions, having children is part of their religious duty. For Jews and Christians, a duty is to 'go forth and multiply' (Genesis), in other words to have children. Most religions see children as a gift from God, a blessing on the marriage. It is as if God has shown his approval of their union by giving them the gift of a child.

So, if this is the case – and even non-religious people can agree with many of those reasons for having a child – why do some women still feel they have to have an abortion? In effect, they are rejecting God's gift (if that is how they see it) or destroying a symbol of their love and relationship. There must be some very good reasons for their decisions. It is true that most women who have abortions feel very badly about the decision they made, and suffer mentally because of it for a long time. Some never get over it. However, they all feel this was their only option, albeit a bad option. Abortion is seen as a *necessary evil*.

Before we look at some situations and you decide what people should do, let's see what the law says.

The law and abortion

The law defines abortion as 'the deliberate expulsion of a foetus from the womb, with the intention of destroying it'. It is different from a miscarriage, which has the same result (that the pregnancy ends without a baby living), because miscarriage is accidental, a turn of nature.

The law in the UK (excluding Northern Ireland) begins by stating that abortion is illegal. It then goes on to say that there are some exceptions.

Abortion can only be carried out if two registered doctors agree that at least one of the following is true:

1 There is a danger to the woman's mental and/or physical health.
2 The foetus will be born with physical and/or mental disabilities.
3 The mental and/or physical health of existing children will be put at risk

The abortion has to be carried out at a registered place, by a registered doctor before the 24 weeks of pregnancy.

A registered doctor is a doctor who has passed medical exams and is recognised by the Medical Council. So a doctor who has been struck off the official list can neither give advice, nor carry out an abortion. A registered place is a hospital or clinic which has registration with the government, and can perform such medical procedures as abortion because of that registration. So any other place is not legal.

Breaking the law carries great penalties for all those involved.

Some scenarios – what do you think?

Before you look through these scenarios, there are some rules. You can't just agree or disagree with any case, you have to explain why you agree or disagree. Also, you have to say what the consequences of each woman not having an abortion are because they are all asking for the abortion, even if they don't feel good about having to do that. Finally, you have to say whether you think they had another reasonable option – and why.

I know you hate having to explain your thinking! Sorry, folks, the exam wants you to do that so you can get better marks. So let's get some practice in...

Rita

I am a carrier of a genetic disease. My baby is at great risk of being born with that disease – the doctors have done tests, and are sure of it. If it is born, my baby will suffer greatly.

Susan

I am fourteen, and pregnant. I am too young to cope with this.

The Basics

1. What do we mean when we say a child is a 'blessing' on a marriage?
2. If children are so special, why do some women seek abortions?
3. Copy and complete this paragraph:

   An_____ is the deliberate ending of a _____, so that the foetus is destroyed. The law in the UK makes abortion _____. There are some exceptions though.

   Two _____ have to agree that one of these conditions is true – the _____ or _____ health of the woman is at risk; the foetus will be born with _____; and that existing children will suffer because of another baby. The abortion has to take place in a _____ place, within _____ weeks of the pregnancy.
4. Explain three situations in which some people would agree with an abortion.
5. Explain your attitude to abortion, using examples to back up what you say.

Leesa

I was raped. This terrible act has left me pregnant.

Isma

My doctors diagnosed me with cancer. They also found that I am pregnant. The doctors told me that I need the treatment if I want to live – it will be too late for me if I wait until my baby is born.

Jane

I am forty-six. The foetus has been diagnosed with Down's Syndrome.

Task

It is very easy to think that a religious person would automatically view abortion as wrong. Check out this website www.rcrc.org for alternative religious views.

Tamsin

I am single, and have no wish to have children, ever. I am pregnant because the contraception I was so careful to use failed. This pregnancy is neither planned nor wanted.

Now you have learnt about the law and why some women choose to have abortions

The Pro-Life argument

Pro-Life is the term we use for those arguments that disagree with abortion – usually in any circumstances. Pro-Life **pressure groups** include ProLife, and SPUC. Since they support the foetus' right to life, their arguments are all in favour of protecting the foetus to ensure it is born.

> *Read these comments and pick out the Pro-Life argument in each one.*

> I believe that all life is sacred, and must be protected. So, abortion is completely wrong.

> God has created life and, as stewards of this world, humans have to protect life.

> Abortion is the murder of another human being. Murder is wrong.

> The foetus can't defend itself – so someone else has to.

> When a foetus will be born with disabilities, we cannot say what the quality of its life would be, so should not decide to forbid it that life.

> The foetus has a right to life, and not to be discarded as if it is just waste.

Some Pro-Life reasoning

What if Beethoven's mother had decided to have an abortion? Beethoven was deaf – and the law allows abortion for foetuses with a disability. We would not have any of his amazing and beautiful music.

What if Einstein's mother had decided to have an abortion? What if Sir Alex Ferguson's mother had?

Any potential life could have grown up to make the same or greater contribution to the world as any of those. We should not deny that life its chance.

ProLife.org.uk

This organisation was set up to 'secure the right to life of all human beings'. It covers all aspects of the 'right to life' argument, including embryo research, euthanasia and abortion. The Alliance believes it can do this by educating people that life should always be respected. They argue that the right to life is the most important and basic of all human rights.

The ProLife Alliance started in 1996 as a registered political party and contested two general elections. It has since deregistered but continues to work primarily in the political arena, lobbying parliament and at grass roots level. A strong area of their work against abortion focuses on the media and public education. They believe that people need to know more about the reality of abortion, and the other options which are available. Their website is www.prolife.org.uk.

Task

Design a leaflet that gives the Pro-Life side of this issue. Make sure it has a clear title, and is attractive to read.
Research a pressure group that is Pro-Life – design an information sheet about that organisation.

 Now you have thought about the Pro-Life arguments

The Pro-Choice argument

Pro-Choice is the term we use for the arguments that defend a woman's right to choose what happens. It is usually associated with supporting the use of abortion, but it is actually about the woman and her right to decide what happens to her body. Since they support the woman's right to choose, the arguments are about the woman, rather than the foetus.

Read these comments and pick out the Pro-Choice argument in each one.

A woman should have the right to decide what happens to her body.

Where a woman is pregnant as a result of rape or incest, it would be wrong to not allow her an abortion.

Some foetuses are so damaged that it would be cruel to allow them to be born.

If having a child is going to put a woman's life at risk, then she should have the right to an abortion.

Up to a certain point, the foetus cannot survive outside the womb, so shouldn't be thought of as a life in its own right.

If we banned abortions, women would still have them but not in a safe way. We need to protect women.

Abortion Rights
the national pro-choice campaign

Abortion Rights is the national Pro-Choice campaign working to protect and extend women's right to choose abortion. Abortion Rights believes that the woman herself is best able to decide whether or not to continue with a pregnancy and that women need to have the option of accessing a safe and legal abortion if that is what they decide to do. Abortion Rights campaigns against restriction in the law on abortion and for progressive improvement, and for the provision of easily accessible, woman-friendly and NHS-funded abortion services. Nationally and through the work of members and thousands of supporters, it campaigns through petitions, publications, public meetings and political lobbying. Much of its work is aimed at making sure the law works, for example, stopping doctors from blocking abortion requests.

Abortion Rights was formed in 2003 from the merger of the National Abortion Campaign and the Abortion Law Reform Association.

Some Pro-Choice reasoning

Imagine you woke up one day to find yourself tied onto a bed in a hospital room. You realise there are tubes attaching you to an unconscious person in the next bed. You demand to know what is going on. The doctor explains that you are the only person who can help that person to live, but they have to be linked to you for nine months, sharing your blood and taking nourishment from you. Would you be happy? Is that fair?

This can be likened to being forced to continue with an unwanted pregnancy. Surely, if you disagree with the hospital example, you have to accept women should be able to have abortions if they want them?

Task

Design a leaflet which gives the Pro-Choice side of this issue. Make sure it has a clear title, and is attractive to read. Research a pressure group which is Pro-Choice – design an information sheet about that organisation.

Now you have thought about the Pro-Choice arguments

What the religions say

Buddhism and abortion ☸

Buddhist texts do not mention abortion. Most Buddhists would not favour abortion as it is seen as taking a life.

Buddhism tells us:

- Life is special and to be protected.
- The First Precept guides us to help others, not harm them, and to reduce suffering.
- Life begins at conception.
- Buddhists should show compassion (loving kindness) and practise ahimsa (non-violence).
- The main factor in the right or wrong of anything is intention.

The first and most important Precept is to not take life. Since Buddhists believe life begins at conception, abortion is killing. Those involved would have created much bad karma, based on their intentions. Abortion does not happen by accident, so the intention breaks the Precept.

Since a person's life is decided by their karma from past lives, it may be that the suffering a life will endure is necessary for their future. By carrying out abortion, we take away the foetus' chance of paying back bad karma.

All Buddhists should show compassion, including to the unborn, and practise ahimsa. Abortion is an act of violence and often doesn't give the foetus any rights, let alone compassion, and so goes against both values.

Having said that, Buddhists do recognise that at times an abortion can lead to less suffering than if the pregnancy went full term, and so accept it in those circumstances.

Christianity and abortion ✝

Many Christians believe abortion to be morally wrong. Some accept it rarely, calling it a necessary evil.

The Bible tells us:

- Life is sacred.
- All humans were made in the image of God.
- God gives and takes life.
- It is wrong to kill.
- God has planned for the life of every single one of us.

These beliefs make Christians say that abortion is usually wrong. It means killing something sacred, which God has created.
Only God has that right and, by allowing abortions, we take that right out of the hands of God.

The Roman Catholic Church is completely against abortion. The *Didache* says 'Do not kill your children by abortion'. In *Vatican II*, it says 'Life must be protected with the utmost care from the moment of conception.'

However, where a woman needs urgent medical treatment, which will also mean the death of the foetus, the Church accepts the treatment. This isn't considered to be abortion.

Protestant churches accept abortion as a *necessary evil* in some cases. For example, many would accept it for a woman who becomes pregnant after rape. However, they stress that great thought has to have been given, and the abortion has to be the absolute last resort.

Exam Tips

In exams, the question that is asking you to agree/disagree with an abortion statement is often really badly answered. Candidates often just go on about abortion, and don't focus on the statement. For each of the statements at the bottom of pages 51 and 52, try to come up with reasons to agree and disagree, including religious ones. Remember the focus is the statement – it is NEVER to argue whether abortion is right or wrong. The underlining will help you.

Hinduism and abortion ॐ

Most Hindus believe that abortion is wrong. However, in India it does happen as Hindus wish to have a male child for religious and cultural reasons, and poverty makes it difficult to manage big families. This situation is slowly changing.

Hindu scriptures tell us:

- Life is sacred and special, so must be respected.
- Those who carry out abortions are amongst the worst of sinners.
- All Hindus should practise ahimsa (non-violence).
- A woman who aborts her child loses her caste.
- Abortion is as bad as killing a priest, or your own parents.

Obviously, Hinduism therefore teaches that abortion is wrong. Hinduism says that the foetus is a living, conscious person, who needs to be protected. Protection is a result of ahimsa and respect. Since we all go through many lifetimes, each time creating karma for the next, when we abort a foetus we prevent that soul from working through a lifetime. This means we block that soul's progress towards union with the Ultimate Reality. It also means we make bad karma for ourselves. Some Hindu scriptures say that those who abort their children will themselves be aborted many times.

Hinduism allows abortion to save the life of the mother, as she does not need the support a motherless child would.

Islam and abortion

Most Muslims believe abortion is wrong. Shari'ah (Muslim) law does allow abortion, but it is still seen as morally wrong. It is a necessary evil.

The Qur'an and Hadith tell us:

- Life is sacred.
- Allah has planned the life of each of us.
- We are all created individually from a clot of blood and known by Allah.
- It is wrong to kill.
- God decides the time of our birth and our death

These beliefs make Muslims say that abortion is wrong. Abortion means killing something which Allah has created, which is special. We destroy Allah's plans for the foetus, and take away Allah's right to decide the time of our death. This is disrespectful.

Muslims dispute when the soul becomes a part of the foetus. Some say at conception; some at 40 days; some at 120 days. For some this creates a period of time when abortion may be allowed, because the foetus is still just blood and cells.

Most Muslims accept that some abortions are necessary. The most common example would be if the woman's life was at risk by or during the pregnancy. The woman's life in this case would be seen as more important to save (because of her existing family and her responsibilities to them).

The rights of the foetus are the most important.

Abortion is murder.

Judaism and abortion

Most Jews would accept therapeutic abortion (for medical reasons), but not abortion to simply remove an unwanted foetus.

Jewish scriptures and law tell us:

- Foetal life, as all life, is special.
- The foetus is 'mere water' until the fortieth day of pregnancy.
- We gain full human status only when we have been born.
- Abortion, under Jewish law, is not murder.
- The emphasis in Judaism is on life and new life, not destruction of life.

Judaism sees a need for abortion, but does not agree with abortion for any reason. Where a woman's life is in danger, even during childbirth, her life takes priority over the foetus, and an abortion can be carried out. Some rabbis have extended the idea of endangerment to include the woman's mental health, for example in the case of rape.

The Talmud points out that the foetus is a part of the woman, not a human in its own right. Assault on her carries a severe punishment, whereas the loss of her unborn child due to that assault results in compensation only. Many rabbis now approve of abortion in cases where there is likely to be severe deformity of the foetus, for example where the mother has had rubella.

Jews are quick to point out that abortion is not acceptable, unless for therapeutic reasons. However, exactly what counts as a therapeutic reason varies depending on Orthodox, Conservative, Liberal and Reform views.

Sikhism and abortion

Sikhism generally does not agree with abortion. It is seen as interference with God's creation.

Sikh teachings and scriptures tell us:

- Life begins at conception.
- All life is special and should be respected.
- Sikhs should not harm others.
- God fills us with light so that we can be born.
- God created each of us, and gave us life; God will also take that life away.

For Sikhs, there is no direct teaching about abortion. Like most things, it is up to the individual to make their own decisions, guided by God. However, abortion is believed to be morally wrong, because life begins at conception and not at birth. In effect, abortion is a form of murder, since the intention to destroy life is there.

Sikhs try to live their life in worship of God, whereas abortion can be seen as going against God; the destruction of God's creation and the opposite of that ideal for life.

When a Sikh becomes a member of the Khalsa, she or he takes vows. These include to never harm others and to do sewa (service to others). Abortion can be seen as going against both of these ideals.

Any <u>woman</u> who <u>wants</u> an abortion should be allowed one.

The <u>quality of a person's life</u> is more important than just being alive.

The quality of life argument

Quality of Life means what someone's life is like. We try to judge whether that life is worth living because of its quality. For example, if a person is quadriplegic and in constant, extreme pain – is their life worth living? This argument is used to support abortion. It claims the quality of life a child would have if born is unacceptably low, so it would be cruel to allow that child to be born in that condition.

Disability

In 2002, only 1900 abortions out of 180,000 performed were for reasons of disability of the foetus – the quality of life argument. This is not a common reason for an abortion. However, the fact that it is used means that we have to think about it – there could be a question with this as its focus, and you need to be ready.

> *Have a look at these situations. In each case, the woman could seek an abortion, and the law would support her. Which ones would you agree with?*

1 Cheryl has been told that scans reveal her baby has not formed properly, and will be extremely badly disabled both mentally and physically if it survives the pregnancy and is born.
2 Sasha has been told her baby will be born with a severe disability because she had an illness in the early pregnancy that is known to affect the foetus.
3 Preeti has been told that her child has Down's Syndrome.
4 Cara has been told that her child's organs have not developed properly, and her child will need many operations once born. It will never have a 'normal' life.
5 Izzie has been told that her child has a hair lip and cleft palate.

> *Let's imagine each woman carries on with the pregnancy and gives birth. Think about these points.*

1 Cheryl's baby could never look after itself. He had to stay in intensive care for over a year after being born, and had many operations. He has to be looked after 24/7, which has made it very difficult for Cheryl and her husband with their other child, Billy, who is four.
2 Sasha's baby was born blind and deaf. She also has quite serious brain damage. She needs a lot of care, and always will. Sasha's marriage broke up because of the stress, and so Sasha looks after her daughter alone.
3 Preeti's son is a very happy little boy, in spite of his disabilities. He went to an ordinary primary school, when he was ready for it.
4 Cara's daughter lived only six months after she was born, in spite of intensive care and several operations. Cara only got to hold her when she was dying.
5 Izzie's little boy had operations to correct his hair lip and cleft palate. The other children at school haven't all been so nice to him though because of his scar.

> *Did this extra information change anything? Does it make a difference what gender the child is? Does it make a difference if they are likely to suffer greatly or die anyway? Do you think any of the women would choose to have an abortion if they thought their child could have a good quality of life? Whose quality of life is this about – mother or child or both?*

The Basics

1 What do we mean by 'quality of life'?
2 Give two situations in which a woman might seek an abortion on these grounds. Explain how these situations are about quality of life.
3 **Poor quality of life is not a good reason for abortion.** Do you agree? Give reasons and explain your answer, showing you have thought about more than one point of view.

Now you know about the quality of life argument

Whose right is it anyway?

This is a very difficult question to answer.

It is perfect for an 'it depends...' answer – because it really does. It depends on the circumstances of the woman (alone, in a loving relationship...?), and it depends on the circumstances of the pregnancy (life or death situation, age...?). Ultimately, the decision has to lie with the mother – it is her body, she has to have the treatment, and she is the only one who truly knows how she feels.

Having said that, there are many people who feel that they should have a say in the choices to be made.

Who do you think might possibly want to have a say in this decision? Look at the people in this picture. What do you think? Morally, should they have a say in this ultimate decision? Or is there another reason they should have a say?

What if...the man is her boyfriend?

What if...the woman has serious mental health problems?

What if...the woman's life is in danger because of the pregnancy?

What if...she is very religious?

What if...the girl is under sixteen?

What if...this was from a one-night stand?

The point of those 'what if's' was to make you see that there is often more to a decision than a simple choice of two options. They probably made you argue a lot, and come up with even more 'what ifs'.

The more you think about it, the more complicated this becomes – until finally you might have to agree that it has to be the woman's decision ultimately.

Task

Now try these evaluative statements as a snowballing exercise (see page 32 if you haven't done one of these before). When you get your page back, you'll see a whole class-worth of ideas. There are several statements so that your class can tackle different ones. You have to collect comments that agree and disagree.

Religions should have no say in the matter of abortion.

The father should always be consulted about abortion.

Medical opinion should over-ride all other concerns about abortion.

Now you have thought about whose decision abortion should be

Alternatives to abortion

The whole of this topic has been about 'abortion or not'. For the exam, you might get asked about an alternative – is there another option?

Check out this table – it tries to help guide you through the alternatives, and suggests some pros and cons (there will be many more). Remember, though, women who have abortions tend to see no other acceptable alternative to the decision they have made, and most often they have thought about those options.

KEEP IT	CHOOSE TO RISK OWN HEALTH/LIFE	HAVE IT 'FOSTERED'	HAVE IT ADOPTED
In this option, you decide to have the baby and keep it, bringing it up yourself.	In this option, you continue the pregnancy, to the detriment of your health, even your death. The baby may or may not be born. An example would be a woman delaying cancer treatment until after the birth, by which time the treatment cannot work.	In this option, you have the baby, but then someone else looks after it – this might be for just a while. An example might be a schoolgirl, whose parents look after the baby until she is old enough or able to. The baby is not legally anyone else's.	In this option, you have the baby, and then give it up for **adoption**. Someone else becomes its legal parent. You lose all contact, unless the baby later wants to find its biological parents.
PROS Child is born, and has a life with its natural mother.	PROS Child might be born and live.	PROS Child is born, and eventually may have a life with mother.	PROS Child is born, and looked after in a loving other family.
CONS Reasons for wanting abortion may have serious impact, such as can't love child properly, blame the child, might be unable to look after it properly.	CONS The child will have either no mother or a seriously incapacitated mother. Existing family more seriously affected.	CONS Self-esteem of child who has been given up. Confusing situation for all.	CONS Child may want to find biological parent later. Mother may find it much harder to give her baby up than she thought.

Task

Of course, without having actual examples it is very difficult to come up with what would be a valid alternative, and what the pros and cons would be. We are back to that individual circumstances thing again.

Have a look at pages 47 and 53. They are all abortion scenarios. Discuss with a partner the options on this page – are any of them better options than abortion in each case? What are the pros and cons for each? Discuss answers as a class.

Now you have thought about alternatives to abortion

Exam practice

AO2 Tips from the examiner

Candidates – that's you – are often really, really bad at answering AO2 evaluative questions on this topic. They go on and on about abortion being right or wrong – whatever the statement! So here are some tips to help:

1 Read the statement carefully and underline the key words – this will steer your brain in the right direction. Make sure you are answering the question set.
2 Write the statement out on your answer page – your brain processes it a bit better, and you are more likely to answer it.
3 Each time you pause when you are writing, recheck the statement, so that you are still answering it.
4 Double check you have agreed and disagreed, whatever your personal opinion is.
5 Double check you have some religion in your answer.

Advice desk

Okay – have a read of these answers below and imagine you are trying to teach other students how to improve in their exams – what's gone wrong? Give them some good advice.

The question was:

Only women should decide about abortion. Do you agree? Give reasons and explain your answer, showing you have thought about more than one point of view. Refer to religious arguments in your answers.

(6 marks)

Zack – No way! What about the bloke? He's the dad, so he needs a say. In fact, if my girlfriend decided to have an abortion, and didn't let me have a say, I can't write down what I'd do to her. Terrible that, whoever wrote that should be ashamed of themselves.

Jake – I don't agree with abortion, so that's wrong. Abortion is murder, which is wrong. None of the religions agree with it either.

Freya – The woman is the one who has to be pregnant for nine months. She has to put up with the morning sickness and everything. She also gets to look after the baby most of the time when it is born. She knows how she feels and what she can cope with – no one else truly knows. So for all these reasons it should be her decision, and hers alone.

Taylor – Of course women should only have abortions. Men can't have children so they can't have abortions. Stupid question really.

These answers could be genuine – the authors of this book have seen their equivalents every year! Zack has only written from one side – his first comment is valid because it offers a second person whose opinion should count. However, he then has a bit of a rant about his girlfriend and the question – neither is relevant. Don't forget, if you decide to criticise the writer of the question, it might be your hard luck to have that person as your examiner! They never, ever write what they really think – they are just trying to get you to argue. He'd have got just 1 mark, by the way.

Jake hasn't even answered the question – he just said about abortion being wrong. He's got no marks!

Freya has written a good answer, but it sticks to one side, and has no religious content. She has restricted herself to 3 marks.

Taylor simply misread the question, or read what she wanted to read. Either way – no marks!

What the grades look like

Let's remind ourselves of that question.

Only women should decide about abortion. Do you agree? Give reasons and explain your answer, showing you have thought about more than one point of view. Refer to religious arguments in your answer. (6 marks)

Now, to get 6 marks you'd have to answer from two points of view. You'd have to give two or three reasons for each side, which you have explained. You'd also have to include at least one religious argument.

Candidates for each grade write in a certain way. That is to say, there are characteristics that can be recognised in each grade. Here we use that evaluative question to showcase the characteristics of grades A, C and F.

	Candidate answer	Comments from examiner
F	I agree, because she has to have the baby. Maybe she should talk to the dad about it.	This is a simple response, with no development. It does make a point for each side of the argument, but only very simply.
C	I agree, because she has to have the baby. It's her body and her pregnancy. She's the only one who really knows what she can cope with. But she should really see what the dad thinks, because without him there'd be no baby. She might talk to her vicar if she's religious.	C grade answers generally give a spread of ideas. They are often light on good development, or one sided. They lack depth or breadth to their answer. They give some religion, but again it lacks development and depth. If quotations are used, they aren't used to their full potential. Reading it, you get the impression that they have a clue, but could have said so much more.
A	Well, it really does depend. If a woman is pregnant because she was raped, then I don't think anyone should be involved in the decision, but her. Similarly, if her life is in danger. The crucial thing is her health and well-being, and she is the one who knows if she can cope. Most religions would support her in her decision in these situations. On the other hand, if she has a partner, perhaps they need to be involved because they are part of the reason why she is in this situation. It might be that they can help her cope, and so she can avoid having an abortion. I also think that people who follow a religion need to involve their religious leaders – even if it is just for advice or to check what their holy book says. They believe in those ideas, and it's part of their life – they follow their beliefs for other things in their life, so should do so for this as well.	A grade candidates provide both sides of an argument, and they include religion. They explain the points they make – often applying the points they make to the statement. There is breadth and depth to their answers – on both sides. Their answers flow, and are easy to read as well – often the examiner can see it is worth five or six marks before they even reach the end of it! Of course, they'll read it all, but the structure stands out, and helps the examiner with their marking.

Learn the DREARER formula for good evaluative responses –

Disagree with the statement.
Reasons why you disagree.
Explanations of some of those reasons.
Agree with the statement.
Reasons why you agree.
Explanations of some of those reasons.
Religious argument must be in there.

> Have a look at some of your answers to evaluative questions. What sort of answers do you give? What does the next level do that you don't?

Now you have had some evaluative response practice

In this topic you need to understand the concepts of **war** and **peace**. You will also need to know the possible causes of war and examples of wars that have taken place. You will look at how modern warfare has changed and the terrible consequences for the victims of war. You will also investigate organisations that work for peace and alleviate the suffering caused by war. You will learn about religious attitudes to war including **Holy War**, **Just War** and attitudes to **pacifism**. You will also need to understand two key ideas which shape religious attitudes to them – *justice* and *sanctity of life*.

> I am a soldier and I believe in the sanctity of life.

> I believe in the sanctity of life. I would never fight in a war.

Paul   Rami

The Basics

1   Match these words and phrases:

War	Making things fair again
Peace	Armed conflict between two or more sides
Pacifism	The idea that life is special, even sacred
Justice	When people live in harmony with each other, not fighting
Sanctity of life	Belief that fighting is always wrong

2   Explain why you think Rami would not fight in a war.
3   Explain why you think Paul would fight in a war.
4   Who do you think is right? Try to give at least two reasons in your answer.

Definitions

War is armed conflict between two or more groups or nations. It involves the use of armies and weapons in a battle to achieve a goal, such as leadership of a country.

Peace is the opposite of war. It is where people live in harmony with each other, and are not trying to hurt each other. *Pacifists* do not believe in fighting a war under any circumstances.

Justice is fairness. It is where all people have equal rights and freedoms and these are protected by laws made by legitimate governments. If someone goes against these rights and freedoms, then they are punished by the law, and things made right again. A war might be fought to gain justice.

Sanctity of life is the idea that all life is valuable and special. It recognises that every human being has a right to life because we are all unique. Religious people believe that God creates all people and this makes human life sacred. A religious believer might refuse to fight because all life is sacred, or they might choose to fight to protect the life of others.

Now you know the key terms for this topic

A world at war

It is a sad fact that, despite our efforts to create peace and harmony, war is still very much a part of life on earth. Throughout the centuries, many thousands of wars have been fought for many different reasons. The Crusades were fought from the eleventh century for nearly 300 years by Christian soldiers who believed they were fighting for God to recapture the holy city of Jerusalem. Across the world, countries have fought each other for power, land and resources. Usually there is no simple, single reason for why a war might take place, but inevitably they have led to misery and loss of life for millions of people throughout history.

Throughout the twentieth century, there have been many conflicts. The First World War (1914–18) and the Second World War (1939–45) saw European nations and their allies fighting for justice and freedom from invaders such as the Nazis. Many nations have fought wars of independence to gain freedom from former colonial occupation. Wars in Vietnam and Korea were waged by the USA who perceived a threat from communism. In Africa, many wars have been fought by rival groups wishing to take control of their country in the absence of legitimate government. Racial and religious differences have also led to genocide and ethnic cleansing becoming a horrific feature of modern wars.

In the modern world, most wars can be categorised as one of the following:

1 Wars between nations – these are conflicts between rival countries or nations. For example: Israel v Palestinians, India v Pakistan, USA v Iraq.
2 Civil wars – these are conflicts between rival groups within a country. For example, Bosnia, Somalia and Sudan.
3 The War against Terrorism – Post-11 September 2001, the USA and its allies have declared war against extreme Islamic fundamentalists, resulting in the war in Afghanistan.

> *Look at some of the reasons people have given for fighting or for not fighting in a war. Can you split them into the two categories? What other reasons can you add?*

For territory, to take back or gain new land.

In self-defence, when invaded, or under threat of invasion.

Life is sacred, it should never be taken.

Wars are too expensive to fight.

To defend a way of life – your own or other people's.

To change the leadership of a country – your own or another.

Wars lead to too much destruction.

Many innocent lives are lost – war isn't limited to a battlefield.

As an allied force keeping an agreement with another country.

The facts of modern warfare...

Since the start of the twenty-first century, the death toll from war reads:

- 42,000,000 military personnel
- 19,000,000 civilians
- 83,000,000 through genocide/tyranny
- 44,000,000 through famine resulting from war.

Visit http://en.wikipedia.org/wiki/List_of_wars_2003-current to see how war is affecting the world today.

The Basics

1 Describe three different types of war. Give an example of each.
2 Give two reasons, which you think are fair, for going to war. Write two sentences to explain each.
3 Give two reasons, which you think are not fair, for going to war. Write two sentences to explain each.
4 **War is always wrong.** What do you think? Explain your opinion.

Now you know something about modern warfare

Religious attitudes to war and peace

Buddhism, war and peace ☸

Buddhism is a religion of peace. Although Buddhist countries have armies, they exist for defence purposes, and as a secondary police force.

Buddhism teaches:

- The First Precept – to refrain from harming others; this is ahimsa, and is a core principle of Buddhism.
- The Noble Eightfold Path – making you consider others, as well as the consequences of all behaviour.
- 'Hatred does not cease by hatred, hatred ceases by love' (Dhammapada).
- 'He should not kill a living being, nor cause it to be killed, nor should he incite another to kill' (Dhammapada).
- 'Peace can exist if everyone respects all others' (Dalai Lama).

The message of Buddhism is one of peace, not war. Buddhists believe their actions have consequences for their future rebirths. It is wrong to harm others, yet soldiers must kill. Buddhists believe all peaceful means must be tried, because war can lead to greater problems than it solves. War is often the result of the Three Poisons (ignorance, hatred and desire), and war also encourages them, whereas Buddhism seeks to get rid of them. The Dalai Lama is the spiritual leader of the Tibetans and his country was invaded by, and made part of, China. He believes the only resolution can be a peaceful one. He won the Nobel Peace Prize in 1992.

Christianity, war and peace ✝

The teachings of Christianity are peaceful. Jesus taught a message of love and Christianity has a strong pacifist tradition. However, many Christians accept that there are circumstances when it is necessary to use armed conflict and will fight in a Just War. No Christian group would support the use of nuclear weapons.

Christianity teaches:

- 'Put away your sword. Those who live by the sword die by the sword' (Jesus).
- 'Blessed are the peacemakers' (Jesus – Sermon on the Mount).
- 'Love your enemies, and pray for them' (Jesus – Sermon on the Mount).
- 'Peace I leave with you, my peace I give to you' (Jesus).
- 'Everyone must commit themselves to peace' (Pope John Paul II).

Christianity is a peaceful religion if we look at the teachings of both Jesus and St Paul. The Kingdom of Heaven is a place of peace and love, not violence and fighting. Most Christians throughout the centuries have believed in living in peace and harmony but are prepared to engage in war to help defend people, restore freedom and hopefully create a greater good. For example, going to war against Hitler in the Second World War.

Many Christians only agree with war in certain circumstances, for example, to repel an invading force. The Quaker Movement however, is an example of a Christian pacifist group today. Its members will not fight in any war. Many Christians disagreed with the Iraq War because they felt the reasons for it were wrong, and that it led to many innocent people being killed. Where Christians accept war, it has to be the last resort after all peaceful efforts have failed.

Task

For the religion(s) that you are studying, use the information provided to create a booklet that explains the religious teachings about war and peace.

Hinduism, war and peace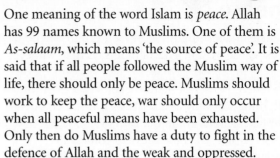

Hindus are split by caste (social division), one of which is *kshatriya* which means 'to protect from harm'. They are a warrior caste. Hindus believe in following dharma (duty), so for kshatriyas fighting is acceptable in Just Wars. However, Hinduism promotes ahimsa (non-violence) and tolerance as key virtues, which are against fighting.

Hinduism teaches:

- Kshatriyas (warrior caste) are expected to be the first to battle, and the bravest in battle; their main duty is to defend and protect others.
- Even an enemy must be offered appropriate hospitality if he comes to your home (Mahabharata).
- Key Hindu virtues include ahimsa (non-violence), tolerance, compassion and respect, as well as protection of others.
- 'The pursuit of truth does not permit violence being inflicted on one's opponent' (Ghandi).
- 'If you do not fight in this Just War, you will neglect your duty, harm your reputation and commit the sin of omission' (Bhagavad Gita).

So, where a war is seen as just, in defence against an invading nation, for example, kshatriyas must follow their duty and fight. Not doing so would gain bad karma, and negatively affect future rebirths. Where it is necessary to protect others, fighting may be the only way, and so is acceptable.

However, Mahatma Ghandi stressed that justice can be achieved through non-violence. Since all life is sacred because Brahman is within all (the atman), war destroys this ideal.

Islam, war and peace

One meaning of the word Islam is *peace*. Allah has 99 names known to Muslims. One of them is *As-salaam*, which means 'the source of peace'. It is said that if all people followed the Muslim way of life, there should only be peace. Muslims should work to keep the peace, war should only occur when all peaceful means have been exhausted. Only then do Muslims have a duty to fight in the defence of Allah and the weak and oppressed.

Islam teaches:

- Greet others *salaam alaikum*, which means 'peace be upon you'.
- Greater jihad is every Muslim's personal struggle to follow Allah, the lesser jihad is Holy War in defence of Islam.
- To those against whom war is made, permission is given to fight (Qur'an).
- Those who die in the name of Allah will be rewarded with paradise (Qu'ran).
- Hate your enemy mildly; for he may become your friend one day (Hadith).

When Muhammad (pbuh) was alive, the Muslims had to defend themselves by fighting. If they hadn't, they would all have been killed. Allah ordered Muslims to fight back when attacked, so Holy War became a duty for Muslims. The Muslim religion realises that sometimes to defend people's rights or to change a terrible situation, we have to fight.

In a disagreement with a nation, if talking fails to solve the problem, it becomes a duty to fight.

Jihad is a word used for Holy War, but there are two kinds of jihad – lesser and greater. The greater jihad is the struggle to always behave in a way that is acceptable to Allah – it isn't about War. Holy War is the lesser jihad.

Task

Working with a partner, write a discussion between two believers: one who will fight in a war and one who says it is wrong to fight. Remember they could both belong to the same religion or to different religions.

Judaism, war and peace ☨

Judaism does not question the right to defend a just cause by war. The Talmud says that 'whoever sheds the blood of man, by man shall his blood be shed'. However, there are rules that exist for fighting war only as a last resort. It is forbidden to take delight in the war or its victory, and Jews believe that when the Messiah comes, all weapons will be destroyed and turned into peaceful tools. Peace remains the ideal.

Judaism teaches:

- The standard Jewish greeting is *shalom*, which means 'peace'.
- Get ready for war. Call out your best warriors. Let your fighting men advance for the attack (Ketuvim).
- The sword comes to the world because of the delay of justice and through injustice (Talmud).
- It shall come to pass...nation shall not lift up sword against nation, neither shall they learn war any more – Nevi'im – about the future before G-d's kingdom is established.
- When siege is laid to a city, surround only three sides to give an opportunity for escape to those who would flee to save their lives (Maimonides Code).

In earliest Judaism, war was a religious duty, and there are many descriptions of wars fought in the Bible. G-d is on the side of the righteous Israelite army, and they win. The Ark of the Covenant was taken into battle with them as a talisman. Today, war is still acceptable, but as a last resort, and only for just reasons, for example, self-defence or when the Jews or Israel are threatened.

There are rules about fighting the wars, including that chances for escape and surrender must be given, that there is no scorched earth policy, and that civilians and prisoners are treated with dignity.

The ideal is peace, and justice is vital for peace.

Sikhism, war and peace ☬

Sikhs have duties to fight for justice and to protect minorities. War should be a last resort, and should be fought in a just manner.

Sikhism teaches:

- The Sikh Khanda includes two swords, and Sikhs wear the kirpan showing a willingness to fight when necessary.
- When all other methods have failed it is permissible to draw the sword (Guru Gobind Singh).
- The Lord is the haven of peace (Adi Granth).
- Peace is believed to come from God.

Several of the Sikh Gurus instructed Sikhs to do physical and military training. Guru Ram Das swapped prayer beads for two swords, showing a stance against oppression and injustice. Guru Tegh Bahadur led the Sikhs into battle for the right to religious freedom. Guru Gobind Singh organised the Sikhs into an effective army after setting up the Khalsa, whose members were prepared to give up their lives for their religion.

Sikhism does not look for wars to fight. Peace through justice is the ideal. However, there is an obligation to fight to get justice where necessary.

Some Sikhs are pacifist out of respect for the sanctity of life.

Task

Hold a class discussion about this statement:
Peace is an impossible dream.

Take a vote at the end of the debate. Which side won? What arguments were the most persuasive?

Fighting a war

Justice is a key idea when we talk about war. Many wars are fought to try to give justice. For example, one country may help another which has been attacked. In some countries, civil wars have occurred because the ruling government is corrupt. The problem with war is that it can lead to *injustice*, because people can get treated unfairly.

There are rules about fighting wars. Most countries have signed an agreement, so they are supposed to follow these rules when they fight. If they don't, they can be found guilty of committing war crimes. These rules are called the *Geneva Conventions*. If people play by the same rules, then everything should be fairer, really.

Captured soldiers – what will you do with them? How will you treat them?

Hospitals in battle zones – will you allow them? Can they be attacked?

Wounded soldiers (captured or on the battlefield) – what will you do with them?

Targets – what is it okay to shoot at or destroy?

Enemy civilians – can you target them? How will you treat them if you capture their town?

Battlefield – what counts as the battle zone?

Weapons – what types are okay to use?

Task

If you had to write a set of rules for war, what would they be? The bubbles at the top of the page will help you think about rules covering all different aspects of war.

Don't forget – all sides in the war have to keep these rules. Think about how you want your soldiers and civilians to be treated.

Thinking about the treatment of prisoners

Civilians and soldiers are captured in war. How should they be treated? Do you treat civilians differently to soldiers? Why?

Look at the ways prisoners of war have been treated. Which do you think are acceptable and unacceptable? Can you give a reason for each decision?

Use of torture for punishment

Use of torture for information

Use of hostage taking

Mass execution

Revenge punishment/execution

Discrimination by sex

Discrimination by nationality and/or race

Discrimination by religious or political beliefs

Political indoctrination

Use as a human shield

Rape, maiming and pillage

▷ **If you thought all of the treatments stated on the left were wrong, you already agree with the Geneva Conventions. Do you think it's a good idea to have rules about how prisoners of war are treated? Why?**

▷ **Look at your set of rules. Do your rules show *justice*? Do they show *sanctity of life*? Will they help deliver *peace*?**

▷ **Research some examples of the abuse of the Geneva Conventions in modern wars. For example, Bosnia, Iraq, Rwanda. Find out how war criminals are tried and dealt with.**

Holy War and Just War

We have seen that all religious traditions believe in peace not war. However, most also accept that there are times when it is necessary to go to war to avoid a greater evil. Within religious teachings there are contrasting views on war, and so religious believers must use their conscience in deciding whether or not they believe a war is morally justified.

There are three possible stances a religious believer may take:

Pacifist – believing all war and killing is wrong.

Holy War – believing it is right to fight a war in the name of God.

Just War – believing it is right to fight a war in the interests of justice and the greater good.

Within some religions there is clear guidance on war.

Christianity

Holy War

> Declare a Holy War, call the troops to arms (Old Testament).

Within Christian history there was once a strong concept of Holy War. In the Old Testament there are many examples of wars fought in the name of God. The combatants believed that God was on their side and indeed had influence over the outcomes of battles. For example, Joshua's army was commanded to blow trumpets to bring down the walls of Jericho. The Crusades (1095–1291) were fought to capture control of the Holy Land. The Christian soldiers believed they were fighting for a sacred and noble cause. They believed that God was with them and the Muslim Turks they were fighting against were the pagan enemies of God.

> It is impossible to conceive of a Just War in a nuclear age (Pope John XXIII).

Just War

St Paul said Christians should obey their rulers, who had been given power by God. When those rulers demanded Christians be soldiers, a compromise had to be found. St Augustine was the first to try, and eventually it was written in detail by St Thomas Aquinas, and is called the *Just War*. The message is clear – sometimes if you don't fight, you allow a greater evil to happen than a war would have caused, so you have to fight.

Christian Just War Rules

1 War must be started and controlled by a proper authority such as a government.

2 There must be a just cause for the war, it must not be aggression towards an enemy.

3 The war must have a clear aim to promote good and overcome evil.

4 War must be a last resort, every effort must have been made to resolve conflict peacefully.

5 It must be winnable, it would be wrong to risk lives with no chance of success.

6 The war must be conducted fairly. Only reasonable force should be used and the risk to civilians minimised.

7 There must be a good outcome and peace restored.

The Basics

1 What do the terms 'Holy War' and 'Just War' mean?

2 Why do you think some religious believers would fight in these kinds of wars?

3 **There can be no such thing as a Just War, because the innocent always suffer.** What do you think? Explain your opinion.

Islam and Holy War

For Muslims a Holy War is a Just War. There are rules for how Muslims should fight a war in the Qur'an, and these were written in more detail by one of the caliphs (rulers). A jihad may only be fought as a last resort and must never be against another Muslim nation.

> *Fight in the cause of Allah those who fight you, but do not transgress limits...if they cease let there be no hostility (Qur'an).*

1 Who fights?
   - Muslims have a duty to join the army and fight, if a just leader begins a war.
   - Not all Muslims have to fight. Muhammad (pbuh) said one man from each two should fight, so that there are still men to defend and look after the towns and villages.
   - Soldiers on the battlefield must fight – running away is wrong, because that makes it more difficult for other soldiers.
   - If a town is attacked, everyone – men, women and children – has to fight back.

2 How is the war fought?
   - It may only begin when the enemy attacks.
   - Civilians must not be harmed, attacked or mistreated. Crops and holy buildings should be left alone.
   - Prisoners of war should be treated well. Money collected for zakat can be used to pay for their food.

3 How does the war end?
   - When people regain their rights.
   - When the enemy calls for peace.

Sikhism and Just War

> *His followers were to emerge as splendid warriors...having taken the baptism of the sword, would thence forward be firmly attached to the sword (Guru Granth Sahib).*

When Guru Gobind Singh formed the Khalsa, it was his intention to create an army of warrior saints committed to the cause of justice. Accepting the need for Sikhs to be prepared to fight, he outlined the teachings of a Just War. In Sikhism this is called *dharam yudh*, which means in defence of justice.

The soldiers were to be *sant sipahi* – saint soldiers. As well as their training, they had an obligation to do *Nam Simran* and meditate daily. In other words, they had to practise their religion devotedly, as well as their military training and preparations. Guru Gobind Singh said: 'Without power, righteousness does not flourish, without dharma everything is crushed and ruined.'

Now you know about Just War and Holy War

War in the modern world

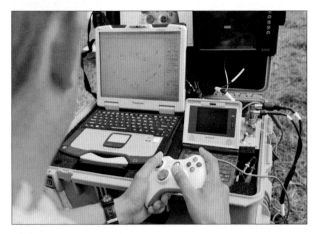

A soldier operating remote military equipment. Has war become a game?

Weapons of mass destruction

Weapons of mass destruction (WMD) are a phenomenon of modern warfare capable of killing and maiming large numbers of people. They can cause massive destruction to both the natural landscape and man-made structures such as cities. It is almost impossible to target only military operations. They are controlled from far away, either in the form of missiles or bombs dropped from planes. So whoever releases the weapon does not experience or see the effect of the weapon face to face. It is very different to soldiers on the battlefield. There are several types of WMD:

1 Nuclear weapons – also known as atomic bombs, cause immediate destruction of all life and structures within their range. The radioactive 'fallout' can have long-term effects.
2 Biological warfare – also known as germ warfare, uses living, disease-causing bacterium or viruses such as anthrax, to cause death or serious illness.
3 Chemical warfare – uses non-living toxins, such as nerve agents and mustard gas, to cause death, incapacity or illness.
4 Radiological weapons – also known as 'dirty bombs', are weapons that use conventional explosives to create bombs that can disperse radioactive material. They kill people, and make the impact area useless because of contamination.

Religious attitudes

Nuclear weapons and other WMD are unacceptable. No religion agrees with their use. They are seen as too extreme and uncontrollable. They do not fit with any Just or Holy War theories, or with ideas of moral behaviour in war.

Religious people believe in the sanctity of life, and so the effects of these weapons go completely against this belief. When the USA used a chemical weapon called Agent Orange in the Vietnam War, thousands of civilians died or were left permanently disfigured by its burning effects. The chemical has also infected the landscape and, more than 50 years on, people are still being affected with birth deformities, cancers and so on.

Religious people also believe that wars should be fought to gain justice for people. These weapons are considered unjust because they arbitrarily kill and maim civilians. During Saddam Hussein's reign in Iraq, his government ordered the use of nerve gas on the Kurds and the Shi'ah Muslims at Karbala. The weapons were being used as a tool of oppression to bring terror upon the people who opposed his rule.

Some religious believers accept the existence of nuclear weapons as a deterrent. They stop others attacking a country, but there is no intention to use them. In other words, they help to keep the peace. Most religious believers, however, think nuclear weapons are completely unacceptable. Even when not used, they cost huge sums of money, which could be better spent. Also, if the technology gets into the wrong hands, there is no guarantee they will not be used. The fact that they exist means they could be used, which is immoral.

> 'Though the monstrous power of modern weapons acts as a deterrent, it is feared that the mere continuance of nuclear tests, undertaken with war in mind, will have fatal consequences for life on earth...nuclear weapons should be banned.'
>
> (Second Vatican Council)

Nuclear War

The effects of the atomic bombs on Hiroshima and Nagasaki

A nuclear weapon has an immense destructive force coming from energy released by a nuclear reaction. On 6 August 1945 the Japanese city of Hiroshima was devastated by the American use of the first atomic bomb in warfare. Over 140,000 people died instantly. Three days later, Nagasaki was bombed. Since then, thousands of people have suffered illness and death from the after-effects of being exposed to radiation.

Today, many more countries have a 'nuclear capability' including Russia, the UK, China, France, Pakistan and India. The increase in the development and possession of such weapons is known as *nuclear proliferation.*

Nuclear Disarmament

For the world to achieve a future without the fear of complete destruction, countries must give up these weapons. This is known as *nuclear disarmament* and is universally recognised as necessary for world peace. This could be achieved by *unilateral disarmament,* where one country gives up its weapons in the hope that others will follow. To date no country has done this, although others, like Japan, have adopted a non-nuclear stance and refused to join the arms race. The alternative is *multilateral disarmament,* which requires all nuclear powers to give up their weapons at the same time.

The case FOR a nuclear deterrent

To discourage other countries from threatening attacks.

They must work because nuclear weapons have not been used since 1945.

Arms agreements can only be reached if the world powers have equal capabilities.

The use of other WMD is made less likely.

The case AGAINST a nuclear deterrent

Nuclear proliferation makes their use more likely not less likely.

Their use could never be morally justified.

They cost the world billions, money which could be better spent on the needs of people.

Other countries are encouraged to develop a nuclear capability.

The Basics

1   Explain, using examples, the term 'weapons of mass destruction (WMD)'.
2   Why do some people think Britain should have a nuclear deterrent?
3   Explain why religious believers could never support the use of WMD.

 Now you know about WMD and the nuclear issue

Terrorism

Terrorism means acts of violence that are intended to create fear. A terrorist is anyone who plans or carries out such an act. Terrorist acts are often directed at civilians and, because of this, many consider them to be unlawful acts of war and violence. The United Nations Security Council regards terrorist attacks as criminal: 'Acts intended to cause death or serious bodily harm to civilians or non-combatants with the purpose of intimidating a population or compelling a government or an international organisation to do or abstain from doing an act.'

In the modern world there have been many recorded acts of terrorism. Al Qaeda's attacks on the twin towers of the World Trade Centre (11 September 2001) and the London Underground (7 July 2005) are just two of the many recorded examples of suicide bombers around the world.

> But why do you think a person would be prepared to die in such a terrible way?

2004 saw the Madrid train bombings carried out by ETA, the Spanish separatist group, killing 191 and injuring 1775. In 1995 in Tokyo the Supreme Truth cult released surin gas in train stations killing 12 and injuring 5000.

Clearly, when people are fighting for a cause they believe in, some will be prepared to go to any lengths to have their voice heard. It has been said that 'one man's terrorist is another man's freedom fighter'. Suicide bombers are an example of the extremes some will go to.

> What do you think about this? Are people who act in this way martyrs?

The Basics

1 What is meant by the terms:
   a 'Terrorism'?
   b 'Terrorist'?
2 Give two reasons why many religious people would consider terrorist acts to be wrong. Explain your reasons.
3 **Terrorism is never right.** What do you think? Explain your opinion.

Terrorist cloud over Olympics

SUICIDE BOMBER KILLS 20 IN MARKET

Tamil Freedom fighters branded terrorists

Victims of landmines

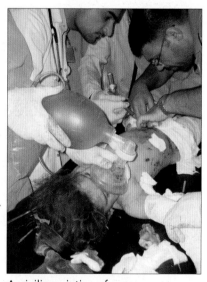
A civilian victim of war

A refugee camp

Now you know something about terrorism

Victims of war

In the modern world, most wars are fought in the less-developed countries of Africa and Asia. Often these conflicts are civil wars fought between rival groups within a country. With the absence of stable government and properly trained soldiers, the civilians in war-torn countries can have their lives shattered in many ways.

Throughout the world there are over 12 million refugees. These are people who have been forced to flee their homes because of fear of massacre, genocide and other violence. Most of these people are forced to seek safety in refugee camps hundreds of miles from their homes, often in neighbouring countries.

Having lost their homes, belongings and livelihoods, refugees often have further problems to deal with. Life in refugee camps is overcrowded with only basic food, shelter and health care. Poor living conditions lead to illnesses such as cholera and dysentery. Many arrive having already been victims of torture and maiming.

Task

Imagine you have been asked to raise funds for a humanitarian aid agency. Design a full-page newspaper advert appealing for funds. Remember, you will need to tell people about why the funds are needed and what you will do with the donations.

The Red Cross and Red Crescent

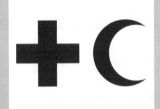

In 1859, a Swiss businessman called Henry Dunant was so horrified by the slaughter he witnessed at the Battle of Solferino that he went to help care for the wounded on both sides. His actions were to lead to the organisation now known as the International Federation of Red Cross and Red Crescent Societies. Over time, the movement has grown into the largest humanitarian aid agency in the world, with a presence in almost every country.

The principle aims of the movement are the relief of pain and suffering for all people affected by conflict. They provide a full range of support to those in need – both immediate short-term aid and also lasting long-term aid. Some of the ways they help include setting up hospitals, establishing refugee camps, providing food, shelter and protection from attack.

The founding principles of the International Federation of Red Cross and Red Crescent Societies are:

1 Humanity – to prevent and alleviate human suffering, to protect human life and health and ensure respect for the human being. To promote understanding, friendship, co-operation and lasting peace.
2 Impartiality – to relieve the suffering of individuals with no discrimination as to race, nationality, religion, class or political opinions.
3 Neutrality – to not take sides in hostilities or take part in controversies and so retain the confidence of all.
4 Independence – the movement will at all times remain independent and national aid agencies that work within the movement must be able to act within its principles.
5 Voluntary service – it is a voluntary relief movement not prompted by gain.
6 Unity – there can be only one Red Cross or Red Crescent society in any one country, it must be open to all and work throughout the territory.
7 Universality – all societies within the movement have equal status, share equal responsibilities and duties in helping each other worldwide.

Find out more at http://www.redcross.int/en.

Also look at the work of Medécins Sans Frontières at http://www.msf.org.uk.

Now you know about victims of war

Peace

Peace is not just the absence of war, but is a state of harmony, where justice exists for all and freedoms are respected. All religions teach the importance of peace on earth and encourage their followers to live peacefully. Throughout history, there have always been people prepared to refuse to use violence or fight in wars, even if it meant they faced imprisonment for their beliefs.

Pacifists believe that all violence is morally wrong. They will not participate in any war, regardless of the reasons for that war. *Conscientious objectors* are people who refuse to participate directly in fighting wars on the grounds of conscience. However, they will assist in non-military ways such as relief work or as medics or mediators.

Working for peace

The golden rule

Buddhism ☸ – I will act towards others exactly as I would act towards myself (Udana-varqa).

Christianity ✝ – Treat others as you would like them to treat you (Jesus).

Hinduism ॐ – This is the sum of duty: do nothing to others which if done to you could cause pain (Mahabharata).

Islam ☾ – None of you truly believe until he wishes for his brothers what he wishes for himself (Prophet Muhammad pbuh).

Judaism ♉ – What is harmful to yourself do not do to your fellow man (Rabbi Hillel).

Sikhism ☬ – As you value yourself, so value others – cause suffering to no one (Guru Granth Sahib).

The Quakers

This is a pacifist Christian group. As a Church they believe they are following the true teachings of Jesus by maintaining a completely pacifist stance. Their Peace Testimony makes clear that they will not use violence in any circumstances. It says that they denounce all violence – whatever its form. They totally oppose all outward wars and strife, and fighting with weapons, for any end, or under any pretence whatsoever. They believe that all relationships should be loving ones, including those between countries. During wars they will mediate for peace between the warring nations. They also do non-combat work such as training to be, and acting as medics for any side, and doing work with refugees and victims of war.

> *Think about these statements. How do they fit with the idea of going to war, or being a pacifist?*

Gandhi

For over 30 years the Hindu leader of India, Mahatma Gandhi, used a policy of non-violence and civil disobedience to oppose British rule in India. His belief in the Hindu concept of ahimsa (non-violence) underpinned his leadership of the Hindus. Through actions such as protests, marches, speeches, sit-ins and hunger strikes, he eventually led his country to independence. He demonstrated that pacifism does not mean you have to just put up with violence and intimidation; when used effectively, it can be as powerful as any physical force.

Dietrich Bonhoeffer

Dietrich Bonhoeffer was a Christian living in Germany during the rise of the Nazi Party. He believed in pacifism and helped found the Confessing Church, which spoke out against the human rights abuses of the ruling Nazis. As the war continued, he felt that he had to be prepared to sacrifice his principles and even his life, because he believed that helping the oppressed was a test of faith. He defied Nazi rule by helping Jews escape the death camps and also worked to overthrow the Nazi Party. Even though he opposed all killing, he was part of a group that planned to assassinate Hitler because he believed it was necessary to do it for the greater good. He was eventually arrested and executed for treason by the Nazis.

Dietrich Bonhoeffer

The Dalai Lama

The Dalai Lama is the spiritual leader of Tibetan Buddhists. He is recognised around the world as a symbol of peace. When the Chinese invaded his country, Tibet, he was forced into exile. However, despite this injustice, he refuses to condone physical fighting against the Chinese. He says that hatred and violence will lead to more hatred and violence. He believes peace will only exist when everyone respects each other. He received the Nobel Peace Prize in 1992. Buddhist monks in Tibet have maintained peaceful protests against Chinese rule, despite being subjected to threats and violence.

The Dalai Lama

Task

Make a PowerPoint® presentation on the theme of peace. You should include what peace means; religious teachings; beliefs and attitudes to peace; and the work of at least one person or group that works for peace. You could also select a suitable song to go with your presentation. Show your work to the rest of your class.

The United Nations

After the devastation of the Second World War, the countries of the world came together on the 24 October 1945 to officially form the organisation we now know as the United Nations (UN). This date is annually remembered and celebrated around the world as United Nations Day. The main aim of the UN is the promotion of world peace. It strives to give all nations a voice in world affairs and to encourage global thinking in the determination of national policies.

This is the headquarters of the UN in New York. Find out more about the UN at http://www.un.org/.

The principles of the United Nations:

◆ To maintain international peace and security.
◆ To develop friendly relations between nations.
◆ To co-operate in solving international economic, social, cultural and humanitarian problems.
◆ To promote respect for human rights and fundamental freedoms.
◆ To be a centre for helping nations achieve these aims.

UNITED NATIONS' CHARTER

WE THE PEOPLES OF THE UNITED NATIONS RESOLVE

☆ To save succeeding generations from the scourge of war, which twice in our lifetime has brought untold sorrow to mankind.

☆ To reaffirm faith in fundamental human rights, in the dignity and worth of the human person, in the equal rights of men and women and of nations large and small.

☆ To establish conditions under which justice and respect for the obligations arising from treaties and other sources of international law can be maintained.

☆ To promote social progress and better standards of life in larger freedom.

AND FOR THESE ENDS

☆ To practise tolerance and live together in peace with one another as good neighbours.

☆ To unite our strength to maintain international peace and security.

☆ To ensure the acceptance of principles and the institution of methods, that armed force shall not be used, save in the common interest.

☆ To use international co-operation to promote the economic and social advance of all peoples.

The Basics

1 What is the UN?
2 Explain the main aims of the UN.
3 Look at the UN's Charter. Make a list of things that could be done to help achieve these aims.
4 Describe the work of the UN peacekeepers.
5 How is NATO different to the UN?
6 Plan an event in school to mark the International Day of Peace.

Peace is the UN's highest calling.

International day of peace

Since 1981, 21 September has been marked out as an international day of peace throughout the world. In introducing this day, the UN resolution called for all nations to recognise and observe this day with a 24-hour cessation in all hostilities and a minute's silence at noon local time. In the UN headquarters in New York, the symbolic Peace Bell is rung to mark the day.

The United Nations Security Council (UNSC)

UN peacekeeper

This part of the UN is responsible for maintaining international peace and security. In the UN Charter it states that the council should work to:

1 Establish peacekeeping operations such as protecting human rights, ensuring aid organisations can function effectively, enabling the conduct of free and fair elections.
2 Establish international sanctions and regimes to prevent trade with nations who the UN have identified as abusing human rights, and to curb the flow of arms to these regimes.
3 To authorise the use of military action to protect civilians in war-torn nations (UN soldiers wear blue berets).

All this is achieved through UNSC Resolutions. In 2007, more than 100,000 blue berets were sent to build and keep peace in nineteen operations around the world. These included Afghanistan, Darfur, Iraq, the Middle East, Haiti and the Congo. The blue berets are made up of professional soldiers from around the world dedicated to the UN ideal of world peace and security.

What do the peacekeepers do?

◆ Monitor the implementation of peace agreements.
◆ Maintain ceasefires to enable political efforts to resolve conflicts.
◆ Help with the creation of stable and democratic governments.
◆ Monitor human rights and security reforms.
◆ Conduct disarmament and reintegration of former combatants.

UN peacekeeping forces are mainly made up of military personnel. However, an increasing number of people with unique skills are being called upon to help, including administrators, economists, police and legal experts, de-miners, electoral observers, specialists in civil affairs and governing, humanitarian workers and experts in communication.

The North Atlantic Treaty Organization (NATO)

One way countries try to create and keep peace is by agreeing to work together towards common goals. These are laid out in documents called treaties. In 1949, 26 countries in North America and Europe signed the North Atlantic Treaty to form NATO. The agreeing nations (*allies*) are committed to supporting each other in protecting their freedom and security using political and military means. So, if Britain were to be threatened by another country, our allies including the USA, France and Germany have agreed to help to protect us.

NATO countries work together to promote democracy, individual liberty, the rule of law and the peaceful resolution of disputes. NATO has helped to end conflicts in Bosnia and Kosovo, as well as having participated in peacekeeping efforts around the world. Find out more at: http://www.nato.int/.

Now you know about peacekeeping forces

Exam practice

Exam Tips

All questions in the exam are written to test your ability to respond to the assessment objectives (AO1 and AO2). You have already looked at tips for AO2 (on pages 44 and 56–57). Let's take a look at AO1.

In AO1 questions you are being asked to show your knowledge and understanding of the topics. The questions will ask you to describe, explain and analyse the information you have learnt.

The AO1 questions will add up to a total of 9 marks. They can be broken up into a range of different mark allocations. There will be short answer questions of just 1, 2 and 3 marks that can be answered in a single word, phrase or short paragraph. Some questions will be 4, 5 or 6 marks and will need you to write longer answers, with more depth.

The 9 marks will be split up in different ways. They might be 1, 2, and 6 marks or 3 and 6 marks or 2, 2 and 5 marks. They will always include a mix of short and long answers.

Make up some exam questions of your own for AO1. Remember they must total 9 marks.

Sample questions

1 mark

1 What is a pacifist?
2 What is terrorism?

2 marks

3 Give two reasons why some countries go to war.
4 What is meant by the term 'Holy War'?

3 marks

5 Describe the work of one individual who has worked for peace.
6 Give three reasons why some religious believers would fight in a war.

4 marks

7 Explain why some religious believers would not fight in a war.
8 Describe the work of one organisation that helps the victims of war.

5 marks

9 Explain religious teachings about holy war.
10 Explain the ways that religious believers might take part in a war.

6 marks

11 Explain why some religious believers would fight in a war. Refer to beliefs and teachings in your answer.
12 Explain, using beliefs and teachings, religious attitudes to peace.

REMEMBER, there will also be AO2 questions on this topic. Here's a couple for you to have a go at:

13 **Pacifists are cowards**. What do you think? Explain your opinion.   (3 marks)

14 **War is never right**. How far do you agree? Give reasons for your answer. Refer to religious arguments in your answer.   (6 marks)

Topic Six Religion and young people

In this topic, you are going to think about how young people relate to religion, and what relevance it has to them. Many young people are brought up within a faith – because their parents follow that faith and think that this is the best lifestyle for them.

So, we'll find out about birth and commitment ceremonies, how young people become religious and then follow a religion, how religion influences their moral development, the problems young people face as they grow up in our society, and the role of schools in developing young people's religious understanding/awareness.

Young religious people

How do religious people bring up their children?

Most people want the same or better chances for their children as they themselves had. If they are religious, they believe in the truths of their religion, which will lead to heaven, paradise, enlightenment or nirvana. For religious people, this is the best possible way to live because it will bring happiness and contentment. So they want their children to follow their religion too.

- They will teach the children *how to live their faith* – how to be a Christian or Muslim, for example, especially in a secular society.
- They will teach them *how to behave* – what the rules are for people of that religion.
- They will make sure they are made *members of that religion* through special ceremonies.
- They will make sure they learn *how to worship*, for example by taking them to their place of worship.
- They will ensure their education includes learning *about their faith.*

Our society is very secular. This means that it doesn't openly focus on religion, and why we should behave in a religious way. Many people don't even practise a religion in an obvious way, even if they follow its principles by treating other people with respect and so on. Many children today are brought up only experiencing religion on rare occasions: for example, festivals, marriages and funerals. For many practising religious people, their home is a spiritual place, and they go to a religious building to carry out an act of worship with others. In a way, this means they have two different worlds to live in, which can make life difficult.

> Do you think it is difficult in Britain today to follow a religion? With a partner, discuss what makes it easy, and what makes it hard.

The Basics

1 Give three reasons why couples choose to have children.

2 Explain how religious parents would try to bring up their children.

3 Why can it be difficult for religious parents to bring up a child in a non-religious society?

4 **Parents should not teach their children their religion until they are old enough to decide to choose it for themselves.** Do you agree? Give reasons and explain your answer, showing you have thought about more than one point of view.

 Now you have thought about religion and young people 75

Birth ceremonies

Buddhism

There are no set religious practices for Buddhists to follow. Any ceremonies that are held come from the culture of the country itself, rather than the religion.

For some families, especially in Theravada Buddhist cultures, they want a monk to come to

bless their child. The monk will visit the home, and chant some religious texts as a blessing. To show their thanks, the couple will give gifts of food, money, or other things to the monk and the monastery he belongs to.

Many Buddhists take their child to the temple soon after it is born. They want to give thanks to the Buddha for their child, so will pray and make offerings of incense, flowers, food and money to show their thanks.

Christianity ✝

Christians have infant baptism, and dedication ceremonies. If you are asked about an initiation ceremony in the exam, you could talk about either. Since there is a little bit more detail in the infant baptism ceremony, we'll look at that.

Don't forget, this ceremony differs between Christian denominations, so you might have experience of a different one.

The parents bring their child to the church to have it baptised. This means it is welcomed into the faith, and made a member through its parents' faith. For Catholics, it also means it is washed clean of sins inherited from its ancestors.

The baby is usually dressed in white, for purity. Everyone gathers around the font for the ceremony.

The priest asks the parents and godparents some questions about their faith, and their intention to bring the

Hinduism ॐ

In Hinduism, there are two very early birth/initiation ceremonies. Hindus in different parts of India will also have cultural ceremonies. There are a number of other ceremonies as well, a little later in the child's life.

The first ceremony is called *Jatakarma*, and happens as soon

after birth as possible. At this time, the father will put a little ghee (butter) mixed with honey on to the baby's tongue. This is in the hope that the baby will have a good nature. The father will also whisper the name of the Ultimate Reality into the baby's ear, so that the baby is welcomed into the faith.

The second ceremony usually happens on the tenth to twelfth day after birth. It is called *Namakarana*, and is the name-

The Basics

Use these questions for each of the religion(s) you are studying (from pages 76-9).
1   What is a birth/initiation ceremony?
2   Describe a religious birth/initiation ceremony.
3   Give two reasons why religious people hold these ceremonies.
4   **Ceremonies held to mark the birth of a baby are just an excuse to have a party.** Do you agree? Give reasons for your answer, showing that you have thought about more than one point of view. Refer to religious arguments in your answer.

They may want the child to receive its name at the temple. Often, in such ceremonies, water is sprinkled over the child. Water symbolises cleanliness and protection from evil. Again, the parents will make offerings as gifts to the Buddha and temple.

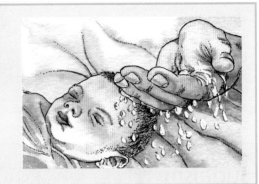

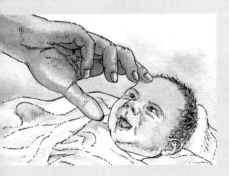

forehead. The cross is the symbol for Christianity, of course.

Then water is poured over the baby's forehead three times – once each for God the Father, God the Son, and God the Holy Spirit. The baby is being baptised in the name of each of these.

In many churches, the family will be given a lighted candle to represent Jesus as the Light of the World. It will be a reminder of

baby up in the faith. Then he takes some water from the font and makes the sign of the cross on the baby's

their promises to bring up the child in the faith.

temple, or a Brahmin priest will come to the home.

An astrologer will read out the child's horoscope, which he has prepared after the child was born, and the name will be announced.

Songs and hymns are sung to show happiness and thanksgiving. Many families will make a fire sacrifice (havan). They offer grain and ghee to the deities through the flames of a fire, whilst

giving ceremony. The baby is dressed in new clothes, and can be taken to the

mantras are being chanted.

77

Islam ☾

There are two main ceremonies – the Tahneek and the Aqiqah.

The Tahneek Ceremony happens as soon as possible after birth.

The father whispers the Adhan into the right ear, then the Iqamah into the left. This means the child has been

welcomed into the faith, and the first things it has heard have been the call to prayer and the name of Allah.

Next, he takes the child and places the soft part of a date on its tongue. This is a hope for the child to be sweet-natured when it gets older.

The Aqiqah Ceremony is the naming ceremony. It will take place a few days after birth. The

Judaism ⋔

Boys and girls have different birth ceremonies in Judaism.

Eight days after birth, a boy should be circumcised as a mark of the covenant between Abraham and the Israelites.

A *mohel* (man trained to carry out circumcision) goes to the home of the child. A special

guest (*sandek*) will hold the child whilst the circumcision is carried out. This person may be a friend of the family or a relative, but carrying out this role is an honour, hence them being a special guest.

The father will read a blessing from the Torah. Then the mohel will bless the child himself, and announce its name.

The baby is then given to its mother to be fed.

Sikhism ☬

As soon as possible after birth, the father will whisper the *Mool Mantra* into the ear of the child. This means it has been welcomed into the faith. He will also put a little honey on to the baby's lips – hoping for a sweet future.

The naming ceremony will take place at the first gurdwara service after birth if possible.

The couple take their child to the service, and with them take the ingredients for karah parshad, and a romalla as a gift for the gurdwara.

There will be readings of thanksgiving from **the Guru Granth Sahib.**

The granthi will stir the amrit with a kirpan, and then drop some into the mouth of the baby. He or she also says a prayer for long life and sweetness for the baby.

The name is chosen next. The granthi opens the Guru Granth Sahib at random, and reads the first word on the left-hand page. The parents use the first letter of

its equivalent weight in money to charity. This purifies the child.

Next, verses from the Qur'an are read out loud, and the child's name will be announced. Again, the father will whisper the Adhan into its ear.

The family will pay for an animal to be sacrificed and its meat given to the poor to say thanks for the gift of a child.

...aby's head is shaved, and the hair ...eighed. The family will give at least

Then everyone will join in a feast to celebrate the birth of the child.

For a girl, she will be announced and named on the first Sabbath after her birth. This happens at the synagogue.

Many Jews follow the *zeved habit* ceremony, where a rabbi will come to bless the baby girl. The family then enjoy a meal of celebration. This happens on the seventh day after birth.

...he family and their guests will then ...elebrate with a party.

this for the first letter of the baby's name. The granthi then announces that name to the congregation.

The karah parshad, which is blessed food from God, will be given out to everyone in the service. The couple arrange for a donation to be given to the poor, as a sign of their thanks to God for their child.

Ceremonies of commitment

Most religious traditions have ceremonies where young people make a personal commitment to their faith. These occur at different times, but usually around the teenage years, so they are sometimes referred to as Coming of Age ceremonies. They mark the change from a child to an adult. After this, young people are expected to take full responsibility for their religious duties.

Buddhism

There is no specific ceremony to become a Buddhist. Some will repeat the Three Refuges in front of others to mark their acceptance of the Buddhist way of life. This is because the Buddha taught that it is the way you live that is important. The believer will simply state, 'I go to the Buddha for refuge; I go to the Dharma for refuge; I go to the Sangha for refuge.'

In Theravada Buddhism, an important ceremony marks a young person's entry into a monastery. Before entering the wat (monastery), the young man must be free from debt and know the Pali phrases he must say in the ceremony. He visits the wat several times and makes gifts of incense, flowers and light, and rings a gong showing he is preparing to join the monastery. The day before the ceremony, he walks in a procession wearing a white robe symbolising his good and pure intentions in becoming a monk. His head is shaved.

On his initiation day, he walks around the wat four times wearing rich clothing and carrying a candle, incense and flower. He takes off the rich clothes and throws coins on the floor, to symbolise the actions of

Christianity †

Around the age of twelve, many young Christians choose to undergo a ceremony of confirmation. This is when they confirm the promises made for them at their baptism. Before the ceremony, there is a time of preparation when they will attend classes, learning what it means to make a full commitment to the Christian faith and how they should live a Christian life.

The ceremony takes place at a special Sunday service, led by a bishop. The bishop will ask three questions: 'Do you turn to Christ? Do you repent your sins? Do you renounce evil?' Each time, the person must answer 'Yes'. The bishop then places his hands on their head and says: 'Confirm O Lord your servant with your Holy Spirit.' This is called the laying on of hands, and at this point the young person receives the blessing of God's Holy Spirit to guide them in their Christian life. The

Hinduism

In Hinduism, sixteen samskaras (special ceremonies) mark key events in a person's life. At around the age of twelve, Hindu boys have a sacred thread ceremony to mark their full entry into their caste. The ceremony happens in a garden around a sacred fire. Puja (worship) is conducted and then the boy's teacher presents him with his sacred thread, which is a series of cotton threads twined together.

The priest, who has taught the boy, then places the sacred thread over the boy's left shoulder and across his body to the right hip. He is now allowed to recite passages from the Vedas and conduct religious rituals. In due

course, he is also now ready for the next stage in life, marriage.

rince Siddhartha when he left the
alace for the last time. He then enters
e ordination hall and asks the
hikkus (monks) to ordain him. He

puts on simple yellow robes to
show that he has left his worldly
life behind. The abbot asks him
questions and he must answer in

Pali. He is then accepted into the
monastery and his religious
instruction begins.

Believer's baptism

In the Baptist Church, they do not
baptise children. They wait until a
young person feels ready to
understand the commitment they
are making. In church, they
announce that they are sorry for
the sins they have committed and
accept Christ as their personal
saviour. The minister then leads
them into the baptistery and dips
them completely under the water.

This symbolises the washing away of
sins and rising to a new life in Christ.

rvice then continues with Holy
ommunion and the newly-confirmed
erson receives the bread and wine for
e first time.

The Basics

Answer these questions for the religion(s) you are studying
(from pages 80–83).
1   Describe a commitment ceremony and explain the
    meaning of any symbolic words, actions and objects.
2   Why do some religious people think it is important to
    have these ceremonies?
3   **Initiation ceremonies are pointless because your
    religion is decided at birth.** How far do you agree? Give
    reasons for your answer, showing that you have
    thought about more than one point of view.

Islam

There are no ceremonies of commitment in Islam, as a child is considered a full Muslim from birth. Islam is a complete way of life and children learn their faith in the family and in the madrasah (mosque school) as they grow up.

The words of the Bismillah mean 'In the name of God, most gracious, most compassionate'

When a Muslim child is four, they have a ceremony called Bismillah. It remembers the first time Prophet Muhammad (pbuh) met the angel Gabriel, when he was commanded to read the first words of the Qur'an from a scroll presented by the angel. The child will have memorised the passage known as the Bismillah and recites it for family and friends to

Judaism

At the age of thirteen, all Jewish boys have a ceremony called Bar Mitzvah, which means 'Son of the Commandment'. In Reform Judaism girls have a ceremony called Bat Mitzvah, which means 'Daughter of the Commandment', and is completed when they are

twelve. These are very important ceremonies because they mark the change from child to adult. From this point, the young person is completely responsible for their religious duties.

There is a period of preparation during which a rabbi will instruct the young person in how to read and handle the Torah, as well as how to perform other religious

Sikhism

When Sikh boys and girls are old enough, they can choose to be initiated into the Khalsa through the Amrit Ceremony. However, it is very common for Sikhs to leave this ceremony until much later in life. Guru Gobind Singh invented this ceremony in 1699 and it involves making a commitment to live by a very strict moral

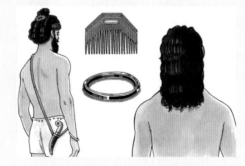

The 5Ks

code, including adopting all of the 5Ks.

The Amrit Ceremony is conducted in front of the Guru Granth Sahib. There are five members dressed to represent the panj piare (five beloved ones). The granthi reads from the holy book and one of the panj piare recites the vows the initiates must promise to keep. The amrit, a mixture of sugar and water, is stirred with a Khanda – double-edged sword. The initiates kneel

hear. They receive gifts of sweets. This marks the beginning of their religious education.

As they get older, they take on more of the religious duties. They learn how to prepare for and complete prayers so that they can fulfil Salah – the second pillar of Islam. Many Muslim children

keep the full Ramadan fast by the time they are in their early teens, thus completing Saum – the fourth pillar of Islam.

obligations such how to wear tefillin. The ceremony takes place on the Sabbath nearest to the boy's thirteenth birthday as part of the usual service at the synagogue. The Torah scrolls are prepared on the Bimah and then the Rabbi calls the boy to read to the rest of the congregation. The boy goes up to the Bimah and

reads the passages in Hebrew for that Sabbath service.

The Rabbi then gives his sermon, part of this is for the boy to remind him of his duty to keep the commandments throughout his life. Finally, the boy is blessed by the Rabbi with the words: 'The Lord bless thee and keep thee.' Then there is a big family celebration.

which means the 'Khalsa is the chosen of God'. Those being baptised reply, 'Waheguru ji ki fateh', which means 'victory to God'. Each person drinks some of the amrit from the bowl, to show equality and the absence of castes.

There are then prayers and hymns and the ceremony closes with the sharing of karah parshad (blessed food). After the ceremony, all Sikh men take the name Singh meaning lion, and

n one knee to show that they are eady to defend their faith. Amrit is hen sprinkled on their eyes and hair o the words 'Waheguru ji ka Khalsa',

women take the name Kaur, meaning princess.

 Now you know about commitment ceremonies

Young people and society

There often seems to be conflict between the older and younger people in any society. Often this appears as elder people criticising the behaviour of young people. This failure of older and younger people to understand each other is known as the *generation gap*. Some of the biggest differences are about music, fashion, culture and politics.

Young people can feel *marginalised* from the rest of society. Teenagers have their behaviour controlled not only at home, but also by local authorities, the law, schools and other institutions. Unsurprisingly, young people often complain that their voices are not heard and that they are criticised unfairly simply because they behave differently from the older generation.

All young people also have to deal with conflicts within their own social groups. *Peer pressure* (influence of people in the same age group) can be difficult to deal with. It can be very challenging for young religious believers. In our society, believing in and living by a religion can seem outdated. Believers may find their friends do not understand why they commit to a lifestyle that prevents them from taking part in some aspects of popular culture.

> *So why do some young people commit to faith if it can be so difficult?*

- Family upbringing and tradition.
- Personal religious experience.
- Enjoy the lifestyle and believe in the religious teachings.
- Gives their life meaning and purpose.
- Allows them to express their spirituality.

> *Why do you think these older people on the right have these negative attitudes of young people? What would you say to each of them to try to change their attitude?*

The Basics

1. Explain, using examples, what is meant by the 'generation gap'.
2. Explain, using examples, what is means to say young people are 'marginalised'.
3. How can 'peer pressure' affect young people today?
4. Make a list of advantages and disadvantages of young people committing to a religious faith.

> *Teenagers today have no respect.*

George

> *I don't like to go out any more; the gangs of young thugs hanging around frighten me.*

Mary

> *Youngsters today have far too much freedom.*

Imran

> *It is too easy for young people today, there is no pressure at all.*

Indira

> *They should have the cane in school. It never did me any harm.*

Bob

> *If we had national service, kids would learn proper discipline.*

Doris

Now you have thought about young people and society

Young people and rights

 Why should I behave like an adult when they treat me like a baby?

Adults think that only their opinions count.

 Why don't we get a say?

I'm old enough to make my own decisions about my life.

I can't wait 'til I'm 18; I'll do exactly what I like!

United Nations' Declaration of the Rights of the Child

1. All children are entitled to these rights regardless of race, colour, sex, language, religion, national or social origin, birth or status.

2. Children are entitled to special protection to enable them to develop physically, mentally, morally, spiritually and socially.

3. A child is entitled from birth to a name and nationality.

4. Children should be protected and provided with enough food, shelter, health care and opportunities to play.

5. Children who are physically, mentally or socially handicapped should have special treatment that meets their needs.

6. Children need love and understanding; they should be cared for by people who can provide them with affection and security.

7. All children are entitled to a free education that will develop their abilities, judgement and sense of moral and social responsibility.

8. Children should be the first to receive relief aid in any disaster.

9. Children should be protected against all forms of neglect, cruelty and exploitation. Children should not work before a minimum age and work should not interfere with their development, health and education.

10. Children should be treated equally and brought up in a spirit of understanding, tolerance, friendship, peace and universal brotherhood.

> Imagine you have been asked to draw up a charter of rights for children. What rights would you want all children in the world to have? Compare your list with the UN Declaration of the Rights of the Child.

> Read the table below. Why do you think the law has decided you have to be a certain age to do some things? What things do you agree and disagree with? Explain your opinions.

> Do you agree or disagree with each of the points? Explain your decision. Is there anything missing? Should all countries have to agree to these rights? In what circumstances might it be difficult to ensure all children have these rights?

Rights of young people in the UK	
AGE	What you can now legally do!
13	Part-time job with restrictions.
14	Enter a pub, but not drink alcohol. Boys can be convicted of rape.
16	Full-time job after June, live alone, marry with parents' consent, ride a 50cc moped, pilot a glider, consent to sex, join armed forces, have an abortion without parents' consent, apply for a passport, drink beer/cider with a meal, buy a lottery ticket, use pumps at a petrol station.
17	Hold a driving licence for most vehicles, pilot a plane, emigrate, cannot be subject to care order.
18	Adult rights in law, vote, get married, buy tobacco and alcohol, open a bank account, see your birth certificate, change your name, serve on a jury, sue and be sued, make a will, place a bet, have a tattoo, buy fireworks, be sent to adult prison.

Task

Read the views of the young people shown on this page. How far do you agree with their opinions? Explain your answers.

Discuss how young people could be made to feel more valued in society.

Now you have thought about children's rights

Young people and school

Faith schools play an important role in the community

TWO-THIRDS OPPOSE FAITH SCHOOLS

Government won't fund more faith schools

The Church was the only provider of education in Britain until Victorian times. It was the influence of the Church on and within government that eventually led to government beginning to set up schools in Britain. Until then, children were simply treated as small adults who were expected to work and contribute to the family income. The Elementary Education Act of 1880 was the first step in making education compulsory for all children.

Today, the lives of young people are very different. Education is a big part of life and schools have a responsibility to prepare young people fully for, not only work, but life in general. School enables children to learn a wide range of skills, to develop socially and psychologically, to explore the world from the security of their classrooms and begin to become the adults they wish to be.

Religion and schools

Historically, religion and schools have been very closely linked as shown above. By 1944, education was compulsory for all children and the government passed an act that made the study of religion in school part of the curriculum for all. Since then, there have been many changes to education in Britain, but Religious Studies has always been part of the curriculum.

Why Religious Studies?

Over the years, the subject of Religious Studies has changed dramatically to take account of the changing face of British society. In the past, Religious Studies concentrated on Christian teachings and beliefs. It assumed all students were believers and often reflected the teaching that happened in church Sunday schools. Today, Religious Studies in schools recognises and celebrates that students come from a wide variety of religious and secular backgrounds. It focuses on key skills and concepts that enable students to learn, understand and question some of the most profound issues facing humankind. It can help us to understand and empathise with people who live life very differently from us. By studying the different beliefs and values of others, it can help us to decide what is meaningful and important. It gives us an insight into the world we live in and our place within it.

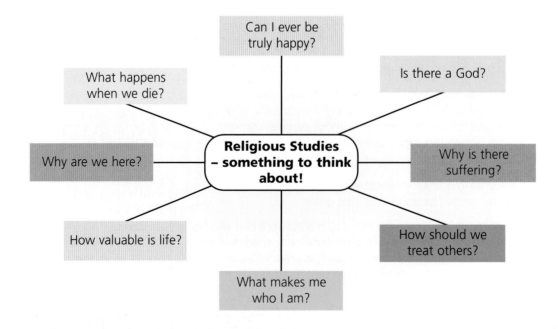

My name is Theresa and I attend the Holy Mother Convent School. As a practising Roman Catholic, my parents felt it was important that I was able to follow my faith in school. I do all the same subjects that my friends at the local High School take, but the ethos of the school is quite different. Most of the girls at my school are also Roman Catholics, but even those who aren't take part in the religious activities in school. Every day we have assemblies that the whole school attends. We sing hymns and always conclude with prayers. Our Religious Studies lessons include preparation for confirmation and begin and end with prayers. They also include study of Roman Catholic beliefs and teachings and help us to understand our personal faith. Our school also has special assemblies when there are important holy days being celebrated, even though we are not on holiday. These sometimes take place at our local church which is good, because it means that we can attend Mass. It was really lovely being in school wearing our ash crosses on Ash Wednesday and not having to worry about being teased or questioned.

My name is Salma. I go to my local High School. As a practising Muslim, I am allowed to wear my hijab, which is a headscarf that covers my hair, although I do remove it for PE. My parents feel it is important that my education includes learning about my faith, so I also attend a madrasah (Mosque School) on Saturday mornings. We have assemblies in school twice a week for each year group. But these aren't like going to worship, usually they include a story with a moral for us to think about, some of them are quite interesting. I like Religious Studies lessons because I get to learn about what my friends believe. In our GCSE course, we have had some great debates about things like the existence of God and arranged marriages. It's really good to be able to hear other people's views and I am confident talking about my beliefs and what they mean to me. Sometimes it can be hard in school practising your faith, not everyone understands that when students are off for Eid, it is an important celebration not 'bunking off'. As a Muslim, I also find the canteen menu very limiting because it doesn't include halal meat. Mostly, however, everyone is very supportive and I was thrilled when some of my classmates also fasted for a day whilst I was keeping Ramadan.

The Basics

1 Make a list of at least ten skills you have learned in school. Choose three of them and say why you think they are important.
2 Give three reasons why you think Religious Studies is taught in schools.
3 In some countries religion is not allowed to be taught in schools. Why?
4 Explain how a faith school may be different to a secular (non-faith) school?
5 **Religion Studies should only be taught in faith schools.** Do you agree? Give reasons for your answer, showing you have thought about different points of view.

 Now you know about religion and school

Young people and religion

Worship

All religious traditions give opportunities for young people to participate in worship. Sometimes there are special services held especially for children and young people. These may include fun activities using dance, drama and popular music. All religions hold classes at their holy building where children can learn more about their religion. Young people can also participate directly in worship. For example, reading from the holy book or helping with the rituals.

Find out more about how young people participate in worship. Make a list of the things they do.

Voluntary work

Many young people get involved in voluntary work in their communities and overseas. Religions teach the importance of caring for others, which might inspire young people to help. They can help in many ways: running youth groups and Sunday schools, visiting the elderly, and taking part in sponsored events. Some young people take a gap year and travel to less-developed countries to work on projects helping to improve the lives of others.

Investigate some of the voluntary work opportunities for young people wishing to take a gap year.

Festivals

Festival celebrations are a fun time. Children learn the stories behind the festivals. They get holidays from school and lots of presents. The celebrations often have a party atmosphere, including fireworks, special food and fun games. They decorate their homes, dress up and spend time with family and friends.

Many young people commit to faith. Some are brought up in a religious family. Others may have personal experiences that make them search for answers to questions they have about life, and religion may help them find these answers. Some young people may be influenced by others such as their friends, teachers or inspirational people. Whatever their reasons, religion can be a big part of their lives.

Social activities

All religious traditions have social activities for all ages. Holy buildings are often designed to include community rooms where all sorts of activities take place. Many young people attend youth clubs and classes at their place of worship. They give a chance to enjoy fellowship with their peers in a relaxed and friendly atmosphere, where their beliefs will be understood and respected.

Make up a weekly timetable of events for a holy building showing the activities for young people.

Research a festival that is particularly enjoyed by children. Write a children's diary entry saying why it was such a good time.

Youth organisations

Lots of young people join youth organisations such as the Worldwide Scout Movement. These groups engage young people in all kinds of interests and help them to develop skills they may not have the opportunity to learn elsewhere. They also include opportunities for them to participate in and learn about faith. For example, in church parades and learning about the beliefs and teachings of fellow scouts around the world.

Find out the principles of a youth organisation like the Scouts or Brigades and how it links to religion.

Religious holidays

Lots of young people enjoy going on special holidays called retreats, organised especially for young people by their community. They mix fun social activities with time for worship and reflection. Many young people like to travel to important places in their faith such as Mecca, Amritsar and Jerusalem. Roman Catholic churches organise trips for young people to help the sick and disabled at Lourdes. Every year, thousands travel to Taizé in France to spend time reflecting and developing their spirituality.

Find out about the activities that take place in Taizé. Why do you think so many young people go?

Task

Pictures are a great help when you are trying to remember things. So collect some images for each of the categories on this page – make your work visually attractive.

 Now you know about youth participation in religion

Exam practice

Exam Tips

Stimulus material is provided to give you clues for your answers so it is worth spending a few moments studying the material provided. In the example below the picture provides a direct link to a couple of the questions. Can you see which ones? How can the stimulus help you to write a good response?

Time test

As you get near to the exam, it is important to practise writing timed answers to the exam question. You need to allow time in the exam to settle down, read the paper and have time to check through your answers at the end of the exam. This means you have about 20 minutes to complete a question. Remember to look at the marks available for each part of the question. They will help you to judge how much you need to write and, therefore, how long to spend on a question. If the question part is worth 1 mark, you don't need to write a five-minute essay!

It is important not to rush through your answers; you do have time to complete them well. It is worth spending a few moments thinking about your answer to a question before actually rushing to write it down. Some questions are only short answer responses and will not take very long. Questions asking you to describe, explain or give opinions and reasons will take more time. These questions will need you to think through your answer first, it might be worth making a few pencil notes planning your response if it's a question you are finding difficult.

> TAKE THE TIME TEST –
> *complete the exam question below
> in 20 minutes.*

Religion and young people

(a) What is the religious element of a school assembly for? (1 mark)

(b) Give **two** reasons why Religious Studies is a subject in school. (2 marks)

(c) 'Religion should only be taught in faith schools.' What do you think? Give reasons for your opinion. (3 marks)

(d) Explain, using an example, how a baby is welcomed into the faith community. (6 marks)

(e) 'Religion is too old fashioned for young people today.' Do you agree? Give reasons for your answer, showing you have thought about more than one point of view. (6 marks)

Sometimes it's easy to write loads more than you need or too little, and to get the question wrong. So here is some guidance to help you with the time test from the previous page.

Question guidance

(a)(1 mark) questions require only a single word, phrase or sentence in response. There are lots of possible ideas here, notice the question asks for an example of a specific aspect of school assemblies, not just anything.

(b)(2 mark) questions ask for **two** reasons so it is important to make sure that the reasons you give are different. It is a good idea to number your reasons and start each one on a new line. Not only does this make your answer clear for the examiner, but it also helps you to make sure you have done what the question asks.

Again, there are lots of possible ideas here. Make sure your answer is based on reasons rather than opinions.

(c)(3 mark) questions are asking for your opinion on an attitude expressed in the statement. You may agree, disagree, be undecided or even have no strong opinions at all. Whatever your response, it is important to remember that your opinion must be supported by reasons. A reason is different to an opinion because a reason can be supported with evidence. There is a difference between emotional opinions and informed opinions. In the exam, you need to write an informed opinion using two or three reasons to be assured of full marks.

(d)(6 mark) questions need you to spend a few moments structuring your answer. You need to write a clear and cohesive account to achieve full marks. Rambling answers can be overlong and cost you time in the exam, they are also not necessarily going to achieve full marks.

In this question you need to write a detailed account of the birth ceremonies in one religious tradition. There are several ways to approach this. One possible way is to think of the response as two paragraphs. In the first paragraph, you describe the ceremony. In the second paragraph, you explain the meaning of symbolic words, objects and actions used in the ceremony.

Don't worry if you can't remember everything, you can still achieve full marks for an answer if it is clearly and coherently written, including some of the main points.

(e)(6 marks) the full evaluation part always comes last in the question. It is worth spending a few moments structuring you answer, and even briefly jotting down a couple of reasons for and against the statement in a plan. You will also need to include reference to at least one religious viewpoint, so it can be worth jotting down any ideas you have for that too. Remember, you are evaluating the attitude expressed in the statement NOT the topic in general.

In this question you are being asked to weigh up whether or not religion is meaningful for young people today. You need to present reasons that both agree and disagree with the attitude. It's a good idea to also include examples to support your reasons. Think about the work you did in this topic on young people and society and young people in religion. It's always a good idea to make sure your break your answer up into at least three clear paragraphs. You should finish by stating what your opinion of the statement is, with a reason or two.

Appendix I

Revision outline

This is a revision guide. It follows the outline of topics in the specification. If you already know all of the answers when you read through it, you will probably do brilliantly.

Use the guide as a checklist of what you know, and what you have still got to get to grips with. You could even use it as a last-minute check before you go into the exam. When you have finished all your revision, you should be able to recognise each word. Each phrase should trigger a whole lot of ideas in your head – definitions, examples and explanations. When it does, you are ready.

TOPIC	WORDS TO LEARN	SUBJECTS WITHIN TOPIC – DO YOU KNOW…?
ONE: RELIGION AND ANIMAL RIGHTS	Animal rights Stewardship Creation Sanctity of life Vegetarianism Companionship Animal experimentation Factory farming Zoos Hunting Fur trade Ivory trade Extinction Cloning Genetic modification	• How humans use animals to help them • How humans exploit animals • How humans and animals differ – the status of each • Religious attitudes to animal rights • Religious attitudes to slaughter methods, to meat eating, and about any food rules • Religious attitudes to animal experimentation • Religious attitudes to zoos, including their role in conservation of species • Religious attitudes to uses of animals in sport, including hunting, bull fighting and racing • Religious attitudes to farming, including factory farming • The 'rights and wrongs' of each of the ways humans use animals

TOPIC	WORDS TO LEARN	SUBJECTS WITHIN TOPIC – DO YOU KNOW…?
TWO: RELIGION AND PLANET EARTH	Creation Stewardship Awe Community Pollution Climate change Natural resources Natural habitat Earth Summits Renewable energies Sustainable development Conservation	• Religious explanations of how the world and life began • How the planet can be a source of awe and wonder, making us think of God • The problem with trying to help humans, but still protecting the environment • How people damage the environment • How and why people help the environment, both as individuals and in groups • The world's response to environmental problems, e.g. Earth Summits, Kyoto, etc. • Religious attitudes to the natural world • Religious attitudes to each specific topic – climate change, pollution, use and abuse of natural resources, destruction of natural habitat, and conservation • How modern living contributes to the problems, and how it needs to be part of the solution
THREE: RELIGION AND PREJUDICE	Prejudice Discrimination Positive discrimination Equality Justice Community Tolerance Harmony Sexism Racism Religious prejudice Homophobia Ageism	• What different types of prejudice there are • Why people are prejudiced • How people show their prejudice • How tolerance, justice, harmony and the value of each person are relevant in this issue • Religious attitudes to prejudice generally • Religious attitudes to all specific types of prejudice – racism, sexism, homophobia, ageism, religious prejudice • How religions respond to prejudice and discrimination • How religions help the victims of prejudice and discrimination • What specific individuals have done to fight racism, and other prejudice • What the government has done to fight prejudice, e.g. the Race Relations Act • What positive discrimination is, and why it happens

TOPIC	WORDS TO LEARN	SUBJECTS WITHIN TOPIC – DO YOU KNOW...?
FOUR: RELIGION AND EARLY LIFE	Abortion Sanctity of life Quality of life Miracle of life Blessing Conception Viability Rights Pro-Life Pro-Choice Pressure group	• When life begins – the different views • Why children are seen as a blessing • What we mean by 'miracle of life' • What we mean by 'abortion' • Why women have abortions • The arguments around 'quality of life' abortions • The law about abortion • Religious attitude to abortion • Examples of when religious believers generally would accept an abortion is necessary • What rights all those involved have or should have – mother, father, foetus • Alternatives to abortion • The work of pressure groups on each side of this issue
FIVE: RELIGION, WAR AND PEACE	War Peace Conflict Justice Sanctity of life Community Pacifism Just War Holy War Victims Peacekeeping force Terrorism Weapons of Mass Destruction Nuclear weapons Nuclear proliferation	• Why religious believers believe in pacifism • The issue of sanctity of life to argue both for and against war • Examples of recent wars, applying Just/Holy War theories to them • How war makes victims of many • Organisations that help victims of war • Why religious believers might go to war • Explanation of Just War, including its rules • Explanation of Holy War, including its rules • Attitudes to war, including teachings/beliefs to support those attitudes • Attitudes to peace, including teachings/beliefs to support those attitudes • How a religious believer has worked for peace • How and why peacekeeping forces work • Attitudes to nuclear weapons, and nuclear proliferation, including beliefs/teachings to support those attitudes

TOPIC	WORDS TO LEARN	SUBJECTS WITHIN TOPIC – DO YOU KNOW…?
SIX: RELIGION AND YOUNG PEOPLE	Birth ceremony Initiation ceremony Commitment ceremony Upbringing Spirituality Moral code Faith group Commitment Belonging Brotherhood Membership Generation gap Peer pressure Faith school Assembly	• Examples of birth ceremonies from each religion you study • Examples of initiation/commitment ceremonies from each of the religions you study • How our upbringing influences our behaviour, beliefs and attitudes • Why young people belong to faith-based groups and organisations, including some examples • How and why young people come into conflict – generation gap, peer pressure, society • The problems met by being a believer as a young person • The benefits found by being a believer as a young person

Appendix II

What a question paper looks like

You will be given a question paper, and an answer booklet in the examination.

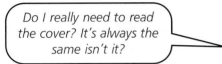

Do I really need to read the cover? It's always the same isn't it?

Well, no they aren't all the same, and it is easy in a stressful time to mix up what you are meant to do. Probably your teacher will have told you a million times what you have to do in the exam, but you can still forget. It is a good idea to just check through the cover – it is like a calming exercise which helps if you are nervous. It also reassures you that you do know what you are doing.

The cover will remind you:

• How long the exam lasts – so plan and use your time well. Reassess after each full question answered – you might have gained or lost time. Don't spend too much time on one question, but don't rush yourself either. You start with four questions to answer in 90 minutes – about 22 minutes a question.

• That you get a choice of any four of the six questions on offer. If you answer them all, you'll be given marks for the best four, but it might not be the best use of your time. Some people find they have lots of time left when they have finished what they should do, so they do extra questions to pass the time!

• That you can choose one or two religions for each question. If you have studied two religions, then it is a good idea to answer every question which asks for religious attitudes as if it was the same question twice, once for each religion. Your answer will be much clearer, and so easier to mark.

• To use blue or black ink/pen. This makes your paper easier to read and mark. This is especially important when exam papers are going to be marked online – you need your writing to be clear and bold, so the examiner doesn't have to struggle to read it.

• That you should do any notes or practice work on either your answer booklet, or on extra paper. Sometimes, people write correct things that they then don't put into their real answer. If you hand in all your working out and notes, the examiner can credit you for anything you missed out. They are obliged to read it all. In your answer booklet, write on the lines only – don't go into the margins or above/below the box. The OMR system which scans your booklet into the computer for the examiner to mark online isn't designed to pick up anything outside the writing area – it might cost you marks.

So much for the cover, what about the inside?

There will be six questions, and the chances are that each one will have a picture or bit of writing to start with. The pictures are meant to stimulate your brain, and start you thinking. In other words, they are meant to help you by triggering the relevant ideas for that question.

In the sample paper on the next few pages, the questions are split 3/6/3/6. There has to be a 3 and a 6 mark evaluative, but the other nine marks could be split up a different way – could be 1/2/6, or 2/3/4, or 4/5, for example. So be prepared (through the practice in this book) for that.

Sample paper

There are six altogether - you should answer four. If you do more, all your work will be marked but you only get marks for your best four.

Answer **four** questions.

There are 18 marks for each question.

1. **Religion and Animal Rights**

    Look at the picture below.

This is the stimulus. The idea is that it helps you with the question, triggering ideas.

(1.1) Give **three** ways in which humans use animals as helpers. *(3 marks)*

Three different ways

Make a comment on rights of animals

Must be animals *helping* or no mark – so 'zoos' isn't clear as helping

(1.2) Explain religious attitudes to animal rights. Refer to beliefs and teachings in your answer. *(6 marks)*

If you studied two religions, answer this question in two paragraphs – one per religion. It makes it easier for the examiner.

(1.3) 'Religious people should campaign against bull fighting'.
    What do you think? Explain your opinion. *(3 marks)*

Should it banned? Everywhere? Whose business is that?

You have to put at least one religious comment in to be able to get more than 3 marks

(1.4) 'Humans should eat more meat.'

    Do you agree? Give reasons for your answer, showing you have thought about more than one point of view. Refer to religious arguments in your answer. *(6 marks)*

It's a good habit to always start with 'It depends...'; then you can put some extra in, e.g. '...if your religion insists you eat meat...'

Need to answer from an 'agree' side and a 'disagree' side. Maximum of only 4 marks if you do one side.

2. Religion and Planet Earth

Look at the picture below.

> **ICEBERGS COLLAPSE: YET MORE EVIDENCE OF GLOBAL WARMING**

Use this in part a.

For this 'Explain briefly...' question you'll have to make three points about climate change. Use examples to strengthen what you say.

(2.1) Explain briefly what is meant by climate change. *(3 marks)*

You'll need to give some religious arguments. You can't just list reasons, you need to explain them too.

(2.2) Explain, using examples, why religious people think they should protect the environment. *(6 marks)*

Give at least four reasons why and an explanation of two or three.

(2.3) 'God can be seen in nature.'

What do you think? Explain your opinion. *(3 marks)*

Is it? You need to say 'Yes, because...' What other problems? What problems might religious people say? Is pollution a bigger problem for some than others?

(2.4) 'Pollution is the biggest problem in today's world.'

Do you agree? Give reasons for your answer, showing you have thought about more than one point of view. Refer to religious arguments in your answer. *(6 marks)*

3. Religion and Prejudice

Look at the statement below.

> **I have a dream that one day little black children and little white children will live together in a world where the colour of their skin does not matter.**
>
> *Martin Luther King*

(3.1) Explain briefly the difference between prejudice and discrimination. *(3 marks)*

> Say what each one is, with an example that shows the difference.

> This word means 'what they have done', it isn't literally 'fighting'.

(3.2) Explain how religious believers have fought against racism. Use examples in your answer. *(6 marks)*

> This starts from the idea that God made everyone – so being prejudiced means insulting his work. Doesn't it depend if there is a God?!

(3.3) 'Being prejudiced insults God.'

What do you think? Explain your opinion. *(3 marks)*

> Use examples (real or made up) to strengthen the points you make. Examples act like explanations – they get marks!

(3.4) 'Only laws can stop discrimination.'

Do you agree? Give reasons for your answer, showing you have thought about more than one point of view. Refer to religious arguments in your answer. *(6 marks)*

4. Religion and Early Life

Look at the picture below. This woman has just found out that she is pregnant again.

Use three reasons most people would agree with: not 'weird' ones – go for the obvious.

(4.1) Explain briefly why some women choose to have an abortion. *(3 marks)*

(4.2) Explain the arguments used **either** by Pro-Life **or** by Pro-Choice in regard to abortion. *(6 marks)*

It is an 'either/or' question. If you answer both, you'll get credit for the better one but you will waste loads of time.

(4.3) 'Sometimes it is wrong even for religious women not to have an abortion.'

What do you think? Explain your opinion. *(3 marks)*

Key word is 'not' – don't misread the question.

(4.4) 'Religion should not interfere in issues of life or death.'

Do you agree? Give reasons for your answer, showing you have thought about more than one point of view. *(6 marks)*

This whole question (a –d) is about abortion, but here you could write about any life or death issue because this part of the question hasn't specified abortion.

5. Religion, War and Peace

Look at the picture below. It shows the medals won by an American soldier in the war against Vietnam. He gave them to a museum in Vietnam as an apology for his part in that war.

Text explains the picture – read it and look at the picture.

(5.1) Explain briefly why some wars happen. *(3 marks)*

Give two or three reasons and put examples as part of your explanation for 'Explain briefly...' questions.

(5.2) Explain religious attitudes to nuclear weapons. Refer to religious beliefs and teachings in your answer. *(6 marks)*

Nuclear, not just any kind of weapon.

(5.3) 'Religious believers always fight for peace.'

What do you think? Explain your opinion. *(3 marks)*

Give two reasons for your opinion and explain them.

(5.4) 'Wars cause more problems than they solve.'

Do you agree? Give reasons for your answer, showing you have thought about more than one point of view. Refer to religious arguments in your answer. *(6 marks)*

Two sides; three reasons per side, two reasons explained per side; make sure there is religious content.

6. Religion and Young People

Look at the following conversation.

> Bill: Hey, Ben – fancy coming to Scouts with me tonight?
>
> Ben: It's at that church isn't it?
>
> Bill: Yeah, we meet there. Have to go to church once a month too. But Scouts is about a lot more than that. Try it.

(6.1) Explain briefly why some young people join organisations within religion. *(3 marks)*

Why they join, not what groups they join.

(6.2) Describe and explain **either** a birth ceremony **or** an initiation ceremony in **one** religion. *(6 marks)*

List the elements of the ceremony, in order. Say what some of them mean or why they happen.

One or the other, not both, and only in one religion. This question expects you to provide a lot of detail to get four or more marks.

(6.3) 'It is wrong for parents to choose a religion for their baby.'

What do you think? Explain your opinion. *(3 marks)*

(6.4) 'Religion isn't relevant to young people.'

Do you agree? Give reasons for your answer, showing you have thought about more than one point of view. *(6 marks)*

END OF QUESTIONS

Glossary

Abortion deliberate expulsion of foetus from womb with the intention to destroy it

Abortion Act (1967) the UK law on abortion, which was amended by the Human Fertilisation and Embryology Act (1990)

Adoption where one/two people take on someone else's child legally as their own

Ahimsa ⊕ ॐ non-violence

Akhirah ☾ belief in Judgement Day, heaven and hell

Allah ☾ One God, Islamic term for God

Animal experimentation use of animals to test products and medicines, and to advance medical knowledge

Animal rights the idea that animals should have rights because of respect for life

Atman ॐ inner 'self'/soul

Bible ✝ Christian holy book

Brahman ॐ Ultimate Reality

Buddha ⊕ Siddattha Gotama, the enlightened one, founder of Buddhism

Climate change global warming, which is characterised by freak and extreme weather, and which is seen as the major issue for the planet

Cloning taking the DNA from something and using it to produce a replica of the original being

Conservation helping to mend environmental damage, or to protect the environment

Creation idea that God created the world from nothing

Destruction causing the loss of something, e.g. cutting down trees which destroys natural habitats

Dhamma ⊕ Buddhist teaching

Disability lack of ability relative to the standard for a group, e.g. most people have no hearing difficulties, so someone who is hearing impaired can be considered to have a disability

Discrimination acting on prejudice

Emissions the release of gases and pollutants into the atmosphere that can cause environmental damage and health problems

Eternal life ✝ Christian concept of life everlasting with God in heaven after this life

Extinction the wiping out of a species, so that none can be found in any surveys over a set period

Factory farming farming as a business, where animals are intensively farmed

Fostering where a person(s) legally looks after someone else's child for a period of time, but do not take the child as their own

Genetic modification changing the DNA of something to be able to change the species, e.g. a pig to make its body parts compatible with humans for transplant; a crop to make it grow more quickly

Guru Granth Sahib ⊕ Sikh holy book

Guru Nanak ⊕ founder of Sikhism

Holy War ☾ conditions under which Muslims should fight war

Hunting chasing animals to kill for food, fur, sport

Jesus ✝ founder of Christian religion; believed to be Son of God by Christians

Judgement Day ✝ ☾ ✡ belief that at the end of time, all humans will be raised from the dead to be judged on the actions of their life by God

Just War ✝ ⊕ conditions under which Christians/Sikhs should fight in war

Karma ⊕ ॐ the consequences of our words, deeds and actions

Kashrut ✡ food laws

Khalifah ☾ stewardship; belief that Allah has given us duty to look after world

Khalsa ⊕ Sikh who has taken vows of faith

Kurahit ⊕ prohibitions ('Do not...') for Khalsa Sikhs

Langar ⊕ Sikh community kitchen, set up by Guru Nanak

Life after death idea that when we die, there is a next life, either through reincarnation, rebirth or Judgement Day (heaven/hell)

Miracle of life idea that getting pregnant, carrying to full term and giving birth is a very special, even miraculous event

Muhammad (pbuh) ☾ Prophet of Islam, final prophet to world (Seal of prophets)

Natural habitats areas of natural vegetation and associated wildlife

Natural resources the things we use, such as coal, gas, oil, which are found naturally

Noachide Laws ☷ early set of laws found in Torah

Pacifism belief that all violence is wrong

Peace absence of war; harmony between groups/ nations

Pollution when too much of something is dumped into the atmosphere, on to land, into water, so that the environment is affected

Prejudice pre-judging someone, usually unfavourably, before getting to know them

Pressure group a group set up to put pressure on society/government to make change, e.g. AbortionRight

Pro-Choice arguments to support a woman's right to decide what happens to her body, e.g. abortion

Pro-Life arguments to protect the right to life, in this book, of the foetus

Poverty deprivation of the basic needs that give quality of life, e.g. food, water, shelter, money

Quality of life argument about what a person's life should be like for it to be worth living, used within abortion debate

Qur'an ☾ holy book of Islam

Racism prejudice based on colour/race

Rights the right to something, e.g. in the case of abortion a foetus' right to life, or the father's right to be involved in the decision

Sanctity of life idea that life is special and sacred

Sentient being idea that all life has sensory ability, i.e. can see, hear, etc

Sexism prejudice based on gender

Shari'ah Law ☾ law of Islamic countries, based on Qur'an, Hadith and Sunnah

Stewardship belief that humans are given the duty/task to look after the world for God; in Islam, khalifah.

Suffering pain and discomfort felt as a result of something, can be caused by nature or by humans

Sunnah ☾ the words and deeds of Prophet Muhammad (Pbuh) collected into a book

Sustainable development developing technologies that can be continued, and which do not cause more long-term harm than good

Tipitaka ☸ Buddhist scriptures, means 'Three Baskets' after three groups of scriptures

Ummah ☾ brotherhood – all Muslims are part of the Ummah

Vegetarianism non-meat diet; those who also do not eat dairy products are vegan

Viability capacity for survival, i.e. when a foetus is likely to survive if born, in the UK at 24 weeks

War two or more sides or nations in armed conflict against each other

Waste unwanted or undesired material or substance produced by human activity, also referred to as rubbish

Zoo place where animals are kept on show for the public to see, most are from other countries and climates

Index